FROM
MOORLANDS
TO HIGHLANDS

A HISTORY OF HARRIS & MINERS
AND
BRIAN HARRIS TRANSPORT

by John Corah

Old Pond
PUBLISHING

ACKNOWLEDGEMENTS

The author would like to express his gratitude to Mrs. Margaret Harris and to Brian Harris. They both gave their full support to this book and were of immense help. Brian's memory of details of events of many decades ago is quite astonishing.

Many ex-employees of Harris & Miners or Brian Harris (or, indeed, of both companies in many cases) gave freely of their time to reminisce about their time as a driver or fitter. Bill Baty and Mick Whiteway were invaluable with their knowledge of the very earliest days of Harris & Miners. Reg Hill, Gordon Bamsey, Bert Long, Alf Harvey, Peter Rees, Gary Ball, Ted Butt, Derek Webster, John Liddicoat, and Derek Hudson all came up with some useful stories.

Nigel Bunt, Records Officer of the Register of ERF Vehicles Society, was of immense help with his detailed knowledge of ERFs and large collection of photographs.

This book could not have happened without any of you and your combined help has made it possible. It has been a wonderful experience to have written this story from listening to some of your experiences; some of which I was privileged to have shared with you as an ex-employee myself. If there is anyone I have left out of these credits then I am very sorry, please accept my apologies.

PHOTOGRAPHIC CREDITS
Those that have kindly supplied photographs for use in this book are credited in the captions. Many have come from collections where the photographer is not known; in this case credit is given to the owner of the collection. Every effort has been made to trace the copyright holder and give due acknowledgement.

First published in 2002 by Gingerfold Publications
Revised and reprinted edition published in 2007 by Gingerfold Publications
Third edition published in 2016 by Old Pond Publishing
Benchmark House
8 Smithy Wood Drive,
Sheffield
S35 1QN

Copyright: John Corah and Old Pond Publishing
ISBN 978-1-910456-28-6

Typesetting by Mark Paterson.
Printed by Replika Press Ltd, India.

ABOUT THE AUTHOR

John Corah was born in Exeter in 1945 and after a boarding school and art college education worked in drawing offices, but the call of the road beckoned and he went into sales for a Lancashire textile company.

His lifelong hobby of restoring vintage cars and commercial vehicles produced an unhealthy interest in lorries, having started driving them in the Territorial Army of which he was a member in the 1960s. In 1971 he did the London to Brighton for vintage commercials in a 1932 Albion and then took the same lorry over the French Alps!

After a shake-up in the textile industry John found himself out of work and so was able to change direction yet again and do what he had always fancied; drive trucks. 1973 saw the start of a period of lorry driving; firstly for an agricultural merchant, followed by a year as an H.G.V. driving instructor before going long distance on artics for a timber haulage company. In 1975 he joined Harris & Miners where he stayed for three happy years, but an offer of a job back in the textile industry was too good to let go, so he once again changed career in 1978. Four years later that company ceased trading and in 1982 John was in exactly the same position as ten years before; redundant!

This was yet another turning point as John decided to use his artistic skills gained in the art college days between 1964 and 1966 and started his own business doing pictorial pub signs and traditional sign writing. It was not long before he started sign writing the fleet of Brian Harris, which he is proud to have done until the closure of the company. Indeed, he signwrote the last vehicle for Brian (a flat trailer) the day before closure was announced. His association with Brian Harris goes back over 35 years; even when back in the textile business he was often seen driving for Brian on Saturday mornings and odd weekends to help out.

John lives in North Tawton with his wife and his hobby, playing with historic commercial vehicles, is as strong as ever. He is regularly seen with a 1949 Leyland Octopus at shows and road runs in summer months. Brian Harris has very kindly lent John one of his tractor units and a stepframe trailer to transport the Octopus to far distant events over the years. John is also once again H.G.V. driving instructing on a part-time basis, having been approached by an Exeter driving school in 2000. Lorries are still very much part of his life and he is also a regular feature writer for commercial vehicle magazines.

DEDICATION

I would like to dedicate this book to my family for putting up with me while undertaking this project. Especially to my wife of 39 years this year. Jenny married a long distance lorry driver and as if that were not enough she is now married to a man who writes about lorries, sign writes lorries, driver-instructs on lorries and plays with vintage lorries! My two daughters Katie and Sally have also been a great support and help.

Thank you.

SECOND EDITION PREFACE

Since publication of the first edition of "*From Moorlands To Highlands*" there has been considerable interest in my book. From the launch in July 2002 it took only a couple of years for it to sell out and become out of print. The following for Brian Harris Transport has exceeded all expectations and Brian himself has been very surprised by the amount of interest in his company. I started writing the book before the closure of the company and it very nearly did not get finished as I thought it would be of little interest as the business had been consigned to history. Yes, Brian Harris Transport is indeed history, but it has not been forgotten.

There has been a series of Corgi Classics models produced based on Harris & Miners and Brian Harris lorries. They have become very collectable with the first ones especially changing hands for several hundreds of pounds. The production team at Corgi Classics has a copy of the book and every so often pick another lorry from the pictures and produce another scaled model. A few years ago they had never heard of Brian Harris. However, the first models sold so well that they have got to know his name very well.

There are two preserved lorries on the scene painted in the colours of Harris & Miners that were never part of the original fleet. The owners of these lorries have asked Brian if they could use his colours; such is the following for a traditional haulage company, especially Harris & Miners. There are also several genuine ex-Brian Harris vehicles in preservation and whenever these change hands they seem to demand a higher price because of their history. Two ex-Brian Harris ERF tractor units are used by their owners pulling low-loaders to carry their traction engines around the steam rallies in the summer months. One tractor unit preserved and now living in Kent was brought back to Devon to be sign-written. Its owner made a six hundred miles round trip just so the lorry could be sign-written by Brian's signwriter! Yes, that's right, me! Brian himself owns a preserved ex-Harris & Miners lorry that causes lots of interest whenever it appears at a show; it is also winning prizes as a result of the high standard of the restoration.

There have also been many magazine articles written about the company since my book was first published; so it seems there is still an appetite for knowledge about what was probably the South West's best loved haulage contractor. My publisher has known of my desire to see the book in print again but has been a little wary to go ahead again. That is until recently. Since there are no copies left to be had anywhere and the publishers have been contacted many times about getting hold of a copy they have agreed to print this second edition. There is an extra chapter in this book along with some more pictures hitherto unseen. So this edition is more than simply a reprint.

John Corah, Bovey Tracey, July 2007.

CONTENTS

INTRODUCTION

There can only be a very few small to medium sized haulage companies in the British Isles with a national reputation within the industry and with such a warm heartfelt appreciation by enthusiasts of road transport. Brian Harris Transport Limited is one such company held in high regard by both. Ask anyone in the country (and of course Scotland) who is connected with, or interested in, road haulage and they will almost certainly have heard the name of Brian Harris and seen the very distinctively liveried red, green, and yellow lorries heading north and south between Devon and Scotland. From Moorlands to Highlands. He operated 31 lorries from his depot in Bovey Tracey, South Devon, with the registered office in Widecombe in-the-Moor, on Dartmoor, from where it all began, and where Brian Harris lived with his mother, Mrs. Margaret Harris. Such is the unique position of the company that Corgi Classics Limited included one of Brian Harris's ERF artics and sheeted flat trailer in their 2001 year range of collectors' models.

Road transport is an evocative subject and a political hot potato. The fuel blockade by farmers and hauliers in September 2000 showed just how the country can be brought to such an abrupt halt so quickly without the movement of goods by road. The railway network could offer no alternative. A small island such as ours depends on a good road network and efficient haulage industry. The argument for putting freight back on the railways is lost. It is simply not a practical means of transport for the day-to-day needs of the country. Railways may be fine for the movement of bulk loads such as quarry products, but for the requirements of manufacturing and service industries the lorry is here to stay.

Just as the railways took over the carriage of freight from the canals in the 19th century, (which in turn replaced the horse and cart), so road transport has largely replaced railways. Each in turn has ousted the other because of improved speed and efficiency, and ultimately cost.

Many towns now even lack a railway station so at some point even goods transported by rail must inevitably end up on the back of a lorry to reach their final destination. The major supermarkets rely almost entirely on lorries to avoid double handling and transhipping of merchandise. Their fleets of artics are a regular and constant sight on our motorways, linking central depot to store. Love it or hate it lorries are here to stay as they are both quicker and more cost effective. In spite of successive goverments' procrastinations and the most expensive diesel in Europe the carriage of goods is not about to leave the roads! The railway network seems hopelessly inadequate at even managing its human cargo. Harris & Miners started life in Widecombe-in-the-Moor, a village without a railway. Brian Harris operated from Bovey Tracey, a town that lost its railway many years ago. The company built its business on the carriage of goods by road from the South West of England to all parts of Scotland, a job it continued to do well into the 21st century. If the railways could have competed then Brian Harris would not have survived for all those years from 1946 to 2001.

This, then, is the story of a family run business started by Brian's father and uncle, Jerry Harris and Sam Miners, in 1946, which holds a unique place within the road transport industry. A fleet of British lorries (practically all ERF) with a very traditional and distinctive livery evolved over two generations. A story I have penned from great affection and considerable first hand knowledge of the company. I have been both a long distance driver for Harris & Miners and for the best part of the last twenty years the sign writer of Brian's lorries. I consider it to have been a privilege to be associated with this company for so many years. I relettered a trailer the day before the closure was announced and covered the subsequent auction three weeks later for "Truck and Driver" magazine. The haulage industry is a sadder place without characters like Brian Harris and good, solid, old-fashioned companies like Brian Harris Limited.

I hope you enjoy this book as much as I have enjoyed writing it!

John Corah, North Tawton, March 2016.

THIRD EDITION PREFACE

Since the second edition appeared in 2007 we have sadly lost Brian Harris and his mother, Margaret, and his beautifully restored 1960 ERF KV has been sold at auction. The first two editions are long out of print and, except for the odd copy turning up on sites such as ebay, it is no longer available. My original publisher retired from the business and sold any remaining books he had to another publishing company. They also have ceased trading. So, as I thought, my days as an author had come to an end; but not quite!

In the last year or so I have often posted pictures on various sites and groups on the computer with interests in classic lorries and transport in general and that is from someone who did not even know how to turn a computer on until comparatively recently. I did not have a computer for the first two editions! As a result of this activity I began to get a lot of feedback regarding Harris & Miners and especially Brian Harris. One such comment was; why don't I start a Brian Harris Transport Group on Facebook? So it was that on Sunday 17th of May 2015, with the help of my son-in-law, a group was formed. It has caused a lot of interest and to date has attracted over 300 members; including many old employees of the Company who have renewed contact with each other and many people with a genuine interest in the Company because of the distinctive livery and because of the man who ran it.

A frequently asked question then became 'where can I get the book from?' With my publisher no longer publishing books I began to look around at the possibility of finding another as I was now convinced that the interest was (and hopefully is) still there. There is also more to tell. So it is that 5m/Old Pond Publishing have agreed to this third edition which includes three more chapters and many more previously unpublished photographs.

I hope you enjoy what must surely be the last edition of 'From Moorlands To Highlands' as we put closure to the story with the funeral of Brian Harris in April 2012 and the auction of the KV 'Happy Wanderer.' Also; a catching up of the present whereabouts of existing lorries once part of the fleet.

Since the publication of the second edition of this book we have sadly lost Bill Baty senior who passed away on the 15th March 2009. Without his help with the history of the early days of the Company, and his many photographs I was able to use, it would have been very difficult. The only other passings, that I am aware of since the second edition in 2007, are ex-driver Warren (Brummy) Piggot, Tony Taylor who died in April 2013 and Ted Butt who died in 2008. There is however, a correction to the first edition on page 23, where I stated that Maurice Gouldthorpe retired after 30 years service. This is incorrect as he was taken ill while 'up the road' and died of a heart attack at home a week later. He had started his employment in the quarry before driving a lorry which he did for 30 years.

This third edition will almost certainly be the last words to be written about the Company and I hope it gives you, the reader, as much pleasure as it has given me in writing it. I would like to thank everyone who has helped with information and for the use of their photographs. It is you who have made this all possible. Finally, I am not the cleverest when it comes to computers (the first two editions were written on a type-writer!) so it is with special thanks to my long suffering daughter, Katie, as without her I doubt any of this would have been possible, at least not in a format acceptable to my publisher!

John Corah, November 2015.

Chapter One

THE BIRTH OF A MOORLAND HAULAGE COMPANY

Most businesses have a humble beginning somewhere and Harris & Miners is no different. The biggest road transport firms have mostly started with one man and one vehicle and many can trace their roots back to the horse and cart. I am not sure about the horsepower in the case of this company, but we certainly start our story with one man and a lorry back in 1936.

Harris & Miners was a Devon concern through and through, with its roots firmly planted in the middle of Dartmoor. Widecombe-in-the-Moor to be precise. However, it is to North Devon that we have to go to start the story. It was in Atherington that one of the co-founders was born in 1910. Sydney Harris was to form a partnership with his brother-in-law, Sam Miners, in 1941 but he had already begun a haulage business in 1936 while living in Bow in mid-Devon. By the time Harris & Miners was on the map no-one knew a Sydney Harris as he was always known as Jerry! So it was then that Jerry Harris bought his first lorry in 1936, a second-hand Dennis for £179. £30 of his own money and £149 from Bowmakers. With this lorry came a 'B' Licence, which gave him the licence to carry customers' goods with certain restrictions.

Any haulier had to have an 'A', 'B', or 'C' Licence to be able to operate and this situation continued for many years after the Second World War. The 'A' Licence was for general haulage; the 'B' Licence was general haulage but with restrictions; and the 'C' Licence for the carriage of your own goods only. The only way to get these licences was to apply to the courts which would invariably be opposed by other hauliers, or to buy a lorry with a licence. Any old lorry would do as the licence was all-important and could be transferred to another.

In 1939 Jerry moved to Widecombe and lodged with his sister, who had married Sam Miners. His new brother-in-law, Sam, worked with his brother Bill Miners in an already established haulage company by the name of W.F. Miners. Jerry joined them as a driver for a while until he branched out on his own again in 1946 and was joined by Sam Miners to form Harris & Miners. Sam left his brother Bill, who continued to trade as W.F. Miners and Sons, and there the relationship between W.F. Miners and Harris & Miners ends. Jerry Harris was not required for war service as a gammy foot, as a result of a previous motoring accident, rendered him medically unfit. H & M started with three lorries comprising two Fords and a Commer tipper. The Fords were V8 petrol engined and the Commer a straight-6 sidevalve. Sand, timber, and fruit from Avonmouth Docks being the main loads in those days.

In 1942 Jerry married Margaret Nosworthy from Venton, near Widecombe-in-the-Moor. In a small village like Widecombe, tucked away on Dartmoor, everyone knew everyone and without private transport and a limited public transport system (the Haytor Bus Service provided by Potters of Ilsington), the social life centered around the village hall for the locals. It was at a Saturday night dance in the hall that the two met. Margaret was a farmer's daughter who was most adept at breaking horses and who prided herself on being able to ride anything. The local nurse had a horse to get round her patients on the Moors which was broken in by Margaret. The wedding reception was held at the Wayside Café in Widecombe after a church service at the Parish Church. The Harvey family then owned the café and offered the reception free of charge as Margaret's mother had been a mother to them after their own parents had died. Jerry and Margaret first set up home in one of the church cottages at Dunstone on the edge of Widecombe. A little further along the road was a row of council cottages in which lived Bill Miners at one end and Sam Miners at the other. In 1943 Brian was born. The Reverend Woods christened Brian at Widecombe Parish Church; he had also christened Margaret and married Jerry and Margaret. In those early days the lorries ran out of Widecombe and the administration remained in Widecombe throughout the life of the company. A small, tightly knit community tucked away on Dartmoor had spawned not one, but two haulage companies. W.F. Miners, (who operated out of Ashburton), and Harris & Miners.

Trago Mills, a large retail outlet near Newton Abbot, stands on the site from where the sand was extracted that Harris & Miners started to haul and keep a lorry or two. Caunters sand pit was also not far from Candy and Company of Heathfield, who were manufacturers of tiled fireplace surrounds and Candy Tiles. In 1947 Harris & Miners got their first long distance customer and started a business relationship with Candy that was to last for fifty years. Up until then all their production had been sent by rail from Candy's sidings at Heathfield, a branch of the Newton Abbot to Moretonhampstead line. Heathfield was also a railway junction with another line going up the Teign Valley to Longdown and on to Exeter. Jerry and Sam went to see Mr. Leffbridge in his office at Candy and were offered a test load of fireplace surrounds on one of their lorries to see if road could compete with rail! That load proved the making of Harris & Miners and not only proved that road haulage was quicker and cheaper than rail (even as far back as 1947), but turned Jerry's and Sam's company into a serious long distance fleet, reaching Glasgow with a load of 'Devon Grate' Candy fire surrounds for the first time in 1948. It took a week to get there but was still presumably quicker than a steam train!

Thus begun a connection between Devon and Scotland that was to be the backbone of H & M for as long as the company operated. Initially the lorries had 'B' Licences for the transport of Candy products anywhere, and general haulage restricted to Devon, Cornwall, Dorset, and part of Somerset; but nobody told them which part! Back loads were found from north of the border and a flourishing two-way traffic developed with many Scottish customers being taken on board. Such became the respect for the company that when Jerry died in 1978 the mourners at the Parish Church in Widecombe-in-the-Moor included many from Scotland, and several again turned up for the auction in 2001. In 1948 Mick Whiteway joined Jerry and Sam as a driver having just left the Army in March. He joined them in the following June having walked from Buckland-in-the-Moor, (Mick's aunt was also a Nosworthy), to Widecombe-in-the-Moor to see Jerry about a job. He was then 21 years old and remained with the company until retiring in 1992. There was, however, a four years break of service from 1950 to 1954 caused through no fault of his own but enforced by His Majesty's government – nationalisation.

Bill Baty was already with the company having started at the age of 19 at the end of 1946. He remained close to the business throughout. He also had a four years gap as a result of nationalisation, and was persuaded back by Jerry Harris in 1954 over a pint at the Rugglestone Inn, Widecombe-in-the-Moor. He became traffic manager in 1960 and left to start his own business when Brian "came off the road" in 1965. He continued, however, to operate from the Pottery Road depot and long after retirement was still doing a bit of driving for Brian on the Transit until closure. Such was the family atmosphere of this little community that no one strayed very far.

A close up of the happy couple on their wedding day in 1942. Jerry Harris and Margaret Nosworthy become Mr. and Mrs. Harris. (photo: Margaret Harris)

Sam Miners in 1949 with a Dodge lorry. This drop-sided lorry was left in brown paint as it was when bought. It must have been pressed into service towing another as the warning on the front wing suggests; towing ECO 90. (photo: Bill Baty)

Michael (Mick) Whiteway joined Sydney (Jerry) Harris after leaving the army in 1948. He left the forces in March of that year and started on Harris & Miners in June. He was 21 years old, which was the only requisite for driving a lorry in civvy street, so was put to work driving this Fordson tipper with V8 side valve petrol engine and 6 volt electrics. (photo: Mick Whiteway)

JOD 501 pictured in 1949. Bill Baty drove this Gardner engined Maudslay and his younger brother, Barry, stands proudly beside it. This lorry was only 2 years old when photographed so it is fairly obvious that paint and signwriting was not yet of importance to Harris & Miners. (photo: Bill Baty)

Barry in 1949 having a go at turning over a 5 LW Gardner. (photo: Bill Baty)

Chapter Two

NATIONALISATION

The considerable post-war building programme to replace houses lost as a result of the German bombing of our cities obviously benefited a lot of businesses up and down the country. New houses built in the 1940s and 1950s all had a chimney and very often more than one fireplace. This was more often than not embellished with a tiled surround and mantelpiece. Candy and Company had never been busier.

Harris & Miners were in the right place at the right time to offer their services to transport their products as an alternative to the railways. As a result the long distance aspect of the business grew rapidly to satisfy demand. Not only was it the finished fire surround that needed delivering but also incoming raw materials were also required from local quarries. Sand, flint, clay and stone are all found close at hand. Jerry was by now regularly driving lorries to Scotland and was very often accompanied by Margaret.

However, in 1950 Harris & Miners were nationalised. The only South Devon transport concern to be taken into public ownership when nationalisation swallowed-up privately owned businesses. The fleet then comprised Dodge, Maudslay, Commers, and a Ford V8 which became part of the newly formed British Road Services with a depot in Newton Abbot, at the top of The Avenue. This site is now occupied by the Fire and Ambulance Station. Jerry was taken on by British Road Services for three months and his drivers, including Mick Whiteway, Eric Whiteway (no relation), and Sam Canon became BRS drivers. Bill Baty first went to Devon General "on the buses" before joining BRS. One of the buses he drove while with Devon General was a 1947 AEC Regal based at the Kingsteighton Depot. I and a friend of mine, Brian Beard, owned this bus in preservation for 25 years and it was once used for a Sunday outing for H & M drivers, including Brian Harris who drove it, to a vintage rally near Yelverton. Sam Miners bought a tobacconist shop in Ashburton. When Jerry had done his contractual three-month stint he went into partnership with Peter Lloyd at Zig Zag Quarry at Kingskerswell on the Torquay Road from Newton Abbot. Sand was what was needed for the post-war housing programme and Jerry was soon busy fulfilling their transport needs. The traffic manager for the local British Road Services in Newton Abbot was Bert Jones who was a co-founder of H.J.T. transport after the end of nationalisation.

In 1954 the road haulage industry was de-nationalised by the government of the day and companies such as Harris & Miners had the green light to start up again. British Road Services did not cease to exist but sold off some of the lorries back into private hands. Bids were asked for from interested parties. To prevent running the prices up by bidding against each other a little group got together to decide who wanted what beforehand. Jerry Harris, Sam Miners, Bert Jones, and Aubrey Saunders from Bow arranged it amongst themselves and they all came away with a good deal!

Jerry and Sam bought back the Commers that had been taken over by British Road Services and acquired three AECs as well. Two were of 1938 vintage and had 7.7 litre engines, and the third was a 1946 with the more powerful 9.6 litre engine. The drivers then included Mick Whiteway, Eric Whiteway, Felix Horrell, John Harvey, and Bill Baty. Sam's son, John Miners, left a career with Lloyds Bank to drive a lorry. Funny coincidence as I worked at Lloyds Bank myself in the 1960s and was a driver for Harris & Miners in the 1970s! A yard was taken over at Mile End, on the Ashburton Road, Newton Abbot, and Les Mann became the fitter doing anything that had to be done outside. Any covered workshops, especially workshops with doors, were still a long way off! Two new Commers joined the fleet in 1956/58 and were driven by Alf Harvey (joined 1/10/58) and Ted Gatland (joined September 1954) who had now added to the growing ranks of employees. UUO 496 and YUO 994 were supplied by Moyles of Paignton and came complete with strengthened headboards for Candy fire surrounds, which were carried standing upright with the first one leaning against the headboard.

Time was always in short supply as ever in the haulage business and the second Commer to arrive (YUO) was sent up the road by Jerry un-lettered. In fact there was very little painting and sign writing going on in those early days. The wheels never stopped turning for long enough! Jerry was still "up the road" himself, but was now more inclined to stay back at the yard whenever he could manage it. This was very often managed by keeping drivers "up the road" and turning them round before they had a chance to get home. Jerry would set off to Scotland with a loaded lorry and find one of his drivers heading south. Jerry would then swap lorries and send the hapless soul back to Scotland again. This was in the days that main roads went through every town and there were no dual carriageways, let alone motorways. The lorries also had a very limited turn of speed so apprehending them coming down from Scotland on their usual route was fairly routine. There were, in fact, two speed limits for lorries in those days. 30 miles per hour if the unladen weight did not exceed 3 tons, and anything over that was known as a '20 miler', with a legal limit of just 20 mph. However, one or two of the drivers got cunning and sometimes managed to dodge Jerry. Mick Whiteway recalls one such occasion when Jerry had got all the way up to Manchester to do a changeover and send Mick back north again. However, Mick was having none of it as he was soon to be married and wanted to get home. He spotted Jerry coming north through Manchester and drove his Ford V8 behind a tram to hide out of the way! Jerry had to complete that trip to Scotland himself and on his return Mick had to have a good excuse ready as to where he was and why he wasn't seen. Another time Mick was not so lucky as he had got all the way to Chudleigh Hill and within 5 miles from home when Jerry appeared with another load and turned him round.

Bill Baty with his AEC Matador at Gretna Green in 1954. (photo: Bill Baty)

In 1954 Harris & Miners bought two new Commer artics. ROD 881 had a petrol engine and ROD 882 (photographed) a Perkins P6 diesel. They were both ordered with R6 Perkins but there was too long a wait for these new engines as the Bedford 'S' type was swallowing up the production. According to Brian it was just as well as the R6 proved unreliable through lack of development. The writing above the windscreen says 'Edna May' after the name of the lorry's first driver's wife. Note the hopelessly inadequate mirrors on extra long mirror arms in an attempt to see past the front of the trailer. Signwriting the fleet was still a thing of the future. The model of this Commer was known as the Superpoise and owed a lot of its design to the Humber car. No heater, no radio, no traffic indicators and 30 m.p.h. on a good day! Mick complained of being overtaken by a bicycle on Chudleigh Hill once and he still had 450 miles to go to get to Glasgow! Photographed at Dunns of Uddington, south of Glasgow, with Mick's wife Ann in the cab. (photo: Mick Whiteway)

A summer scene of happy men at work. Bill Mortimore is in the centre of this picture who started with the Company in May 1958 which helps to date it. (photo: Bill Baty)

A pair of Commer two-strokes in Smith Street, Falkirk, in 1958. YUO is a slightly younger version than UUO with the wider grill fluting. It was also unlettered. There being no time as it had to 'get up the road'. A subtle difference in the way Jerry and Brian did things, as in later years J.C. would be called in to signwrite a name plate before a lorry was allowed to leave the yard! The Rootes TS3 (Tilling Stevens, 3 cylinder) two-stroke opposed piston diesel of 109 h.p. was fast and efficient but lacked engine braking and the very distinctive noise it made finally heralded the end of its production, too noisy to satisfy the authorities in more modern times. Ted Gatland and Alf Harvey drove these two. (photo: Unknown)

VDV 241. Bill Baty with his 8 year old son, Billy, in the yard in 1958 in front of the 1956 Albion he drove from new. An unusual coach built cab with fibre-glass front panel. Powered by an Albion oil engine developing a mere 93 b.h.p. with double drive. It was regularly loaded with 16 tons, so Scotland must have seemed an awful long way away with only that power; and it only had a 4 cylinder engine! (photo: Bill Baty)

A Road Haulage Association gathering in Falmouth in 1960. Jack Gregory is the chairman and among the assembled company are many prominent haulage contractors of the day. Two to the right of the chairman in the light coloured suit is Gerald Vallance with Jerry Harris standing behind him. Others in the group include Peter Richard of Richards and Osborne, Len Mathews of Heavy Transport, Bill Miners (far right), Jim Eggbeer, Derek Good, Nick Gross, Bill Stoneman, Harold Witton of Wittons of Collumpton, Bill Tucker and Jeff Hawker. (photo: Margaret Harris)

Chapter Three

THE ACQUISITION OF BLUE WATERS IN BOVEY TRACEY – A NEW DEPOT IN POTTERY ROAD

The whole of the Bovey Basin is clay. It has been mined and extracted for centuries and is still exported all over the world. Clay is used in all sorts of industries as well as pottery and ceramics. Food manufacture and cosmetics to name but two. The potteries around Stoke-on-Trent were (and presumably still are) big users of china clay, which became a regular run for Harris & Miners. Much of the clay from English China Clays at Kingsteignton was transported by H.J.T. Transport (they closed in 2000 after 49 years trading) and Eggbeer's Transport did a lot (and do a lot) for Watts, Blake and Bearne clays. Harris & Miners always worked closely with these two hauliers and had an excellent working relationship with them. Eggbeer's are still very much in business.

The clay pits and mines in the area spawned a lot of local industry including many potteries. One of which was the Bovey Pottery where records show it was visited by Josiah Wedgewood in 1775. The industry was centered around Pottery Road where from about 1840 there were 16 kilns and over 250 workers. Bluewaters was the original clay pit supplying the pottery, and lignite was also extracted for the kilns. There were many underground mines for both clay and lignite from this pit and the site contained a building with a horizontal waterwheel for pumping water out of the mines. Cottages for pottery and mine workers were built in Pottery Road and a thriving community evolved. At one time it was the largest pottery in the Southwest, but by the 1940s it had all but ceased.

Bluewaters had long since flooded and the combination of clay and lignite deposits gave the water its blue colour, hence the name. This derelict site was bought by Jerry Harris and Sam Miners in 1957 to establish a transport depot for Harris & Miners for the life of the company. Sam still had the tobacconist shop in Ashburton where the drivers' wages were delivered each week for the men to collect. With the availability of raw materials and the wherewithal to shift them (from Zig Zag quarry), Jerry and Margaret had a new bungalow built in Widecombe-in-the-Moor. A site was found on the site of an old Army Nissen hut and building began in 1954. Brian and Margaret remain there to this day.

The facilities in that yard in the early days remained extremely basic (see the aerial photograph of 1968, some 11 years later), but things got done just the same. I have to say that over-investment on the yard was never a cause of cash flow problems! The original lorry workshop utilised the building under which was, (and is), sited the waterwheel. There were no doors and only half a lorry could be got undercover due to a lack of space, and Les Mann, who was still the fitter, had to cope with a dirt floor. At least he could now get out of the rain for half a lorry's length! After complaining about his lot the floor was eventually concreted. When the work was completed explicit instructions were given to keep lorries off the new surface for a day or two. That night a lorry was driven onto the new concrete and sank into it. The next day Les Mann left. Mick Whiteway was asked if he would "go in the workshop" and so started his many years looking after the fleet until he retired on 3rd October 1992.

Sam Miners, who was never a fit man, died in 1958 when only in his forties. Uncle Sam, as he was known to Brian, left a widow Daisy Miners and son John. John branched out on his own with a couple of Ford lorries and neither he nor his mother had anything to do with the day-to-day running of Harris & Miners, although they had a financial interest in the company and the land in Pottery Road. Jerry was now in charge and Brian joined his father having just left Ashburton Secondary School aged 15.

As has already been suggested there was never a great deal of money invested in the yard; to begin with there was not even a telephone on the site. Any communication with head office at Widecombe was done from a public telephone box a few hundred yards up the road at Thorns Cross! On one occasion Mick took the van they had at the time to the 'phone box to order some parts and walked back to the yard without it. The next time somebody wanted the van it was nowhere to be seen until a search found it sitting at Thorns Cross. In fact Mick Whiteway and Bill Baty had convinced themselves it had been stolen and it was only a visit to the 'phone box to report the theft to Jerry that revealed its whereabouts! In 1962, after 5 years of enduring the elements, the openings in the building were blocked up and a door installed in the gable end. Jerry had complained one day that there was a cold draught in the workshop to which Mick replied that it might be something to do with a lack of a door! Bill Baty was a keen enthusiast of American Jeeps and many spares he had accumulated lay buried beneath the workshop floor. The waterwheel is there somewhere but before it was buried Mick and Bill took the phosphor bronze bearings off it and sold them for scrap. The whole area is littered with mine shafts and the burial sites of various vehicles.

Bill Baty was the instigator of a telephone line being installed in the yard in about 1960. His job of running the traffic office without one meant several visits a day to the 'phone box to talk to Jerry at Widecombe, and to speak to the drivers all over the country! He got seriously fed-up with that system and took it on himself to have a line installed. "Bloody hell son", was the reaction from Jerry when he saw it, but he soon realised the benefits of a telephone in the yard and it was not long before a second line was installed. As a result the business kept on growing and the work both to and from Scotland as plentiful as ever. In fact, the traffic south from north of the border was so busy every week that getting lorries up there to cover the work was always a concern. Jerry had sometimes been in the habit of sending part-loaded lorries to Scotland just to get them there. Bill had other ideas and would fill up the Sunday shift lorries with multi-drops as the drivers had all day Sunday to get a good way north. Watching for the law became second nature to them as speed limits for lorries was still only 30 miles per hour and most towns had to be gone through. Jerry did not condone speeding and thought 45 miles per hour to be utterly reckless! "Go on steady my son" was his phrase, but of course great distances had to be covered just the same, as Scotland pre-motorway was a long way.

A job that Bill picked up was clay from Watts, Blake and Bearne to the Governcroft Pottery in Glasgow at £4 per ton. £40 for 10 tons which successfully undercut the railways. Even by 1960s prices, £40 to take 10 tons from Devon to Scotland was not dear. However, it got another lorry up there for the many customers Harris & Miners now had for loads coming south. By now a customer base had been established that remained loyal for the next forty years. India (Dunlop) tyres from Inchinnon to Southampton every week. Rayburn cookers to wholesalers in Devon and Cornwall, Allied Ironfounders of Falkirk, Gourock Rope of Port Glasgow, Tullis Russel Paper of Markinch in Fife, Smith Anderson of Lesley in Fife, Munro of Aberdeen, Ridgeways of Dundee, McKinnon of Kilmarnock, Smith's of Darvel, G.R. Stein, and Caperboard to name just a few.

Brian started on long distance for his father in 1960 aged 17 with an Albion Chieftain which was just under 3 tons unladen, the maximum weight that was permissible to drive before being 21. UTT 601 was new in 1956. Two Thames Traders followed that lorry; 363 GTT was the first one, which was also got down to below 3 tons unladen. In 1963, when he reached 21 the second, heavier Trader was bought. Also, in 1960, the first ERF ever to appear on the Harris & Miners fleet was bought new. 373 FOD came complete from Sandbach and Mick Whiteway was sent to the ERF works in the town to fetch it. He took a brown envelope with him from Jerry containing the payment for the lorry and while it was out on test he was given a meal. On leaving for Devon he was given 10/- for something to eat on the way back. This 5LW Gardner powered

4-wheeler had a Boalloy cab and a gross weight of 14 tons. Dick Barrs drove it for twenty years until they were both pensioned off. Ted Butt started with the company when this lorry was new and drove it for a while in its later life, and so did I.

Mick Whiteway became the longest serving employee (he started in June 1948) when Bill Baty left in 1965, (he had started in 1946). Brian had been driving for a few years now on regular runs to Stoke-on-Trent and Scotland. In those days of trunk roads Stoke-on-Trent was a good 8 hours driving time if all went well. A second hard days work would achieve Blackwood, 20 miles south of Glasgow, and deliveries would start on the third day. The following three days getting back to Devon made a tough, six-day week. The lorry then had to be unloaded and loaded again, which left very little time off before going back "up the road". However, Brian was taking more interest in running the business and Bill decided it was time to move on. He applied for a 'B' Licence to start up with a lorry of his own which was rigorously opposed to by practically all the hauliers in the area, (not though, by Jerry or Brian), including Rich's of Crediton who ceased trading many years ago. After a court appearance the licence was granted and Bill bought a new Commer tipper from Moyles of Paignton for lime spreading.

567 PTA, Tom Pearce, photographed in Carlisle on the 16th March 1966. A 1963 AEC artic and drop-side 4 in line trailer. A Park Royal cabbed Mercury with AV470 engine rated at 112 b.h.p. This lorry came to an inglorious end as it was an animal on the road. Alf Harvey jack-knifed it as did Ted Butt. Finally Brian said 'park it round the back and burn the bastard'. (photo: John Henderson)

When Bill Baty left Harris & Miners in 1965 he bought this Commer from Moyles of Paignton to go on lime spreading for Charles Maidment. He later turned it into a tractor unit and went on distance work. (photo: Bill Baty)

CTA 745C, Harry Hawke, drop-side Commer 4-wheeler fully loaded at Carlisle 31/3/65. Seen carrying a spare wheel; a practice that was dropped in later years. (photo: John Henderson)

Chapter Four

BRIAN TAKES OVER THE OFFICE IN 1966

Brian's Thames Trader, 932 MDV, was only three years old when Jerry took Brian off the road and put him in the office to run the traffic. He returned from a trip with it and parked it up in the corner of the yard by the road for all to see. It never turned another wheel until being dragged out following a successful bid of £250 at the closing down auction in 2001, forty-five years later. Even in its short working life it had done many miles on long distance and was often vastly overloaded. 13 tons being noted on one occasion!

A nucleus of loyal drivers now made up the workforce with Mick Whiteway and Alf Harvey in the workshop. Alf joined the company on 1st October 1958 and drove one of the Commer two-strokes. He remained with Brian until retiring in 1991. Ted Gatland drove the other and he started in September 1954. Ted also stayed until he retired over thirty years later. Bill Mortimore (Strutter) had now been employed by Jerry since May 1958 and was still there over thirty years later until a hip operation that was not a complete success brought about early retirement. Bill's job in later years was as yard foreman and shunter driver which is as I remember him during my stint as a driver in the latter half of the 1970s. The faulty hip meant he could no longer get up into the cab of a lorry and although he had run the office in Brian's absence from time to time (such as his trip to the States), there was no such job available at the time he left on disability grounds. Maurice Gouldthorpe came along in 1957 and after thirty years' service he died of a heart attack at home a week later. Ted Butt came from Whiteways Cider in 1960 and clocked up forty years on the books; the last few as part-time, well after retiring age. Several drivers came 'on the books' during the 1960s who remained until they retired or until closure. One or two left for one reason or another and came back again a year or so later. Tony Taylor joined in 1964 and Peter Rees in 1966. Gordon Bamsey in 1964 (rejoined in 1983) and Reg Hill in 1968; he also left briefly and returned to stay until the end. Derek "Birdseye" Webster clocked up over thirty years (with a brief break of service) and his older brother Jimmy started in 1970 and had twenty-five years with the company before retiring. He too did a bit of part-time driving after finishing, as did Tony Taylor. Ted Saunders and Ken Sims both started with Brian in the 1960s and stayed with him until retiring in the 1990s. These two drivers both originated from Devon but lived in different parts of Scotland for many years. Ken in Fife, and Ted in Lanarkshire did the job the other way round and were usually heading north at the end of the week!

One of the odd things dictated by the regulations of the day during the years following de-nationalisation was that a replacement lorry put on the fleet could be not more than half a ton heavier (unladen weight) than the one it replaced. Several of the earlier lorries owned by Harris & Miners were under 3 tons unladen such as the Fords, so the new ones were only slightly bigger. Until this piece of bureaucratic non-sense was rescinded expansion to a bigger, heavyweight fleet was necessarily a gradual process. However, it did nevertheless happen and a letter from Steels Commercials (Exeter) Limited of the 29th December 1966 addressed to Brian sets out details of new Boden and Dyson 28 foot long tandem axle trailers. Delivery for the Dyson would be 8-10 weeks and the Boden "around 3 weeks at present". Delivery would be able to meet the delivery date of a new Leyland Beaver tractor unit due for April 1967.

The specification for the Boden trailer was 28 foot by 8 foot, with tandem axle for a tractor unit operating at 30 tons gross weight. 2 foot 6 inches kingpin position with 3-line air pressure braking system. 9.00 – 20 14 ply India tyres were specified as was a 4 foot 6 inch headboard and 1 foot 6 inch high quadruple drop sides. Supplied in works primer for £1,252.0.0 Delivery from Oldham amounted to £17.0.0. Len Moores signed the letter as Sales Manager.

The folder from Steels Commercials in which was included this quotation had printed on it some names to conjure with. They were main agents for Albion and Leyland and distributors of Guy. They were Boden Trailer Distributors as they were for Clayton Dewandre. They supplied Regent Oils. In February 1968 Steels Commercials quoted Messrs. Harris & Miners of Higher Mills, Pottery Road, Bovey Tracey, for a Leyland Retriever tipper. The question of part exchange was addressed with £1,400 being offered for a 1965 6-wheel Dodge tipper. Delivery for the new Leyland being 2 to 3 weeks for chassis and cab. The specification was for a 15' 9" wheelbase 22 tons gross 6-wheel tipper with 6-speed overdrive gearbox and Leyland 600 engine of 9.8 litres; £4,230.0.0 Spare wheel and carrier amounted to an extra £78.10.0. and delivery to Exeter from ex-works Leyland added another £27.0.0. A Tiverton light alloy 21' body was quoted at £932 and the tipping ram (front mounted) came to £331. Painting and sign writing extra.

In February 1969 the same company put in a price for a 34' trailer of 8' 2" width by Boden on 10.00 – 20 tyres operating at 30 tons gross, for £1,216. 1969 was the year the new plating and testing regulations came into force which meant the workshop facilities at Pottery Road would have to be upgraded. A ramp was built in the yard, as there was no pit in the workshop. New, purpose built workshops with two pits (as opposed to the makeshift shed being used up until 1969) were constructed next to the new ramp. On 16th February Mick and Alf moved in. A toilet and shower was also built on the end of the original shed near the ramp. This ramp was to be able to get under lorries for inspection and cleaning prior to the new annual test, but it could also be used for loading machinery and tractors onto trailers, which meant backing a trailer up to the ramp by the toilets. The first 40' trailer appeared at the end of 1969 and needed a lot more space to manoeuvre. The toilets got knocked into and shaken about many times over the following thirty years! The forklift had to be utilised on one occasion to put the roof back on and in retirement Bill Baty was required to rebuild the wall several times.

That original 40' trailer to appear on the fleet was a York for 32 tons gross operation and went behind a new AEC Mandator, PDV 523G. An old plating certificate issued in 1969 for an ERF unit, 222 TDV, which was new in 1964 shows a maximum train weight of 24 tons. That lorry pulled a 1963 Scammell semi-trailer with a gross weight of 23 tons. 222 TDV had a 150 Gardner fitted and was driven by Maurice Gouldthorpe. It had a rare cab with deep doors, finishing at the bottom of the front wings.

I mentioned a trip to the States earlier in this chapter which needs recording. It happened in 1982 and was organised jointly by Cummins and ERF to visit the Cummins factory in Columbus, South Carolina. Brian was invited along with other prominent users of Cummins engined ERFs. Tony Knowles' father, of Knowles Transport in Cambridgeshire was remembered as being one of the others to go. Because Brian had such a hands-on approach running his business it was difficult for him ever to get away from it. Anyway, get away from it he did and he was gone for two weeks. Bill Mortimore took over the traffic office with Margaret Harris and the two bookkeepers manning the paperwork back at Widecombe-in-the-Moor. John Edworthy was with Brian until August 2001 and Bob Full retired when the firm closed in March 2001.

Bill did an excellent job running the yard in Brian's absence and the store (warehouse built next to the new workshop) was practically emptied of deliveries waiting to get to customers. Brian had a lovely habit of keeping customers' eagerly awaited goods in store for days (weeks sometimes), until they were ringing up to find out where their delivery was. Brian's response was usually surprise that it was not already there as the driver had left days before! He seldom had. However, Brian obviously enjoyed the experience in the States but could not let go and forget the daily problems back home. He was constantly on the 'phone to Bill enquiring how everything was going. On one such conversation Bill mentioned that Ted Butt had a problem with his Commer/Dodge on the M5. Bill could sort it without any doubt and the 'phone call ended. Within minutes Brian was ringing again to conduct operations from the other side of the Atlantic!

Jerry and Margaret with son Brian on his 21st. birthday in September 1964. (photo: Margaret Harris)

Jock Addison and Brian in front of Jerry Harris' new Humber. Jock was a driver for Jerry in the 1960s and then spent several years in Australia. He returned to drive for the Company once again and stayed with Brian until closure. (photo: Bill Baty)

Outside the Rugglestone Inn, Widecombe, in about 1966. Left to right are Bill Baty's father, Bill Baty, Brian Harris, Billy Baty, Jerry Harris and Bill Miners. (photo: Bill Baty)

Brian Harris (in the cab) takes delivery of OUO 340G in 1968 from salesman Albert Molyneaux. An AEC Mandator/Boden trailer. There were two Mandators on the fleet and this was the first lorry the author drove on his first day with the Company in 1975. (photo: Nicholas Hurne)

A lovely black and white publicity shot for Frank Tucker who supplied this 8-wheel tipper to Harris & Miners in 1968. It was registered LUO 638F and named 'Widecombe Lad'. Gordon Bamsey drove this lorry when new. When Jerry Harris first saw it he said what a ridiculous size it was; "far too big to get in anywhere". It was the first 26 ton tipper that ERF made and had a Jennings body. For many years a picture of this lorry adorned the foyer of ERF at Sandbach. (photo: David Corkery)

EDV 893D, 'Dan'l Whiddon', at Carlisle on the 16th. of March 1963. (photo: John Henderson)

Chapter Five

BRIAN HARRIS TRANSPORT LIMITED. A CHANGE OF NAME

In May 1978 Jerry Harris died leaving a widow Margaret, and son Brian, to carry on the business. I had left their employment just two weeks before and gone to Manchester to join another firm, so could not be at the funeral. My parents went in my stead and told me that such was the respect in which Jerry was held that it seemed half the haulage companies of Scotland were represented. The Parish Church of Widecombe-in-the-Moor was packed, as was the Old Inn in the village square afterwards. The tower of the church lacked a clock and as a memorial to Jerry, Brian and Margaret donated a new chiming clock, now fitted high in the tower. A lovely gesture.

Brian was now able to buy out the Miners family and their interests in the business of Harris & Miners, and he formed a limited company in the name of Brian Harris Transport Limited, with his mother as co-director. For some years the Miners family had had no direct involvement in the running of the company, but until now had a share of the property and land. The fleet now consisted of 18 vehicles in the name of Harris & Miners and one blue 4-wheel Seddon tipper in the name of Brian Harris. This lorry in Brian's own favoured blue was nothing to do with Harris & Miners and ran as a separate company. This is where the idea for blue liveries first came from and from then on there was always a blue lorry on the fleet. At the time of closure there were three in two-tone light and dark blue with the usual Wexham Red chassis. The first noticeable change was the appearance of 'BRIAN HARRIS' on the headboards on top of the cabs and as the fleet was repainted or replaced, then the Brian Harris livery gradually replaced Harris & Miners. By the time I started doing any of the sign writing for Brian in 1981 there were still a few in H & M lettering, but they were now fast disappearing.

Brian did not exactly inherit the eighteen strong fleet from his father as he had largely been running the company since coming off the road in 1965, and during the 1970s was responsible for buying new lorries, although Jerry kept a watchful eye for as long as he was able. When Brian bought a new Seddon tractor unit in 1975 Jerry was heard to say, "what do you want that rubbish for?" Brian's answer was that it was cheap, tractor and trailer for less than £8,000. Two were bought at the same time, one by Brian and the other by Roy Butt who was then trading as Mistleigh Transport and who (with his son) now trades under his own name and runs two Scania drawbar outfits from the Teign Valley.

ERF was by now beginning to dominate the choice of lorry, the first one having been bought in 1960 and remained Brian's property until his death. Gardner engines were the favoured power units of the '70s and were fitted in all the ERFs as well as the Guy Big J (180) and the one S80 Foden (240) on the fleet. The Seddon had a 220 Cummins with Fuller Roadranger 10-speed that had a thirst almost unquenchable. I drove it for a few weeks and I remember it doing not much more than 5 miles to the gallon. It sounded all-powerful, but was gutless and incredibly noisy inside the cab, it also shook itself to pieces. I was continually tightening the self-tapping screws that held what passed for cab trim in place. However, it lasted ten years in service and survived well into the mid-1980s, by which time it had even sprouted a Jennings sleeper conversion. Sleeper cabs started to appear in 1978 (shortly after Jerry died, as he would not tolerate them) as Jennings conversions on the 'A' Series ERFs. They were little more than a shelf which needed cutting the back of the passenger's seat off to get the bunk in. Still, it was better than nothing and the drivers had started to demand them. Brian could also see their advantage, as his lorries were where he wanted them in the mornings, instead of parked on a lorry park outside drivers' digs miles away. These digs were also disappearing rapidly as sleeper cabs became the norm. The first of the 'B' Series ERFs to join the fleet in 1976 were also converted from day cabs in 1978, but from then on were delivered with sleepers. There was a conversion available for the Foden, but Brian jibbed at the cost, so a sort of tin structure was tacked onto the cab, which became "Jimmy's nest" as Jim Webster had the dubious privilege of driving it at the time. Reg Hill had it new in 1977 and complained of a wheel wobble at certain speeds, which could only be overcome by steering it from one side of the road to the other! I did a 'Scotch' with it once, which was the only time I had experienced a 12-speed Foden gearbox. An acquired taste!

Other lorries that made up the numbers then included most English makes except Atkinson. As Brian had begun to favour ERF the Atkinson marque never appeared until many years later when he bought a pair of second-hand Seddon Atkinsons with the Leyland DAF 95 cab (F and G registered), which promptly rusted away at an alarming rate. Leyland, AEC, Albion, Dodge, Commer, and Ford all appeared as well. 4,6, and 8-wheelers, artics with flat trailers, tippers, drop-siders, and flatbeds made up the mixed traffic fleet which were practically all on distance work. A Ford Transit flatbed truck went to the Orkneys in 1976 and during that dry summer of 1976 a Series 2 Land Rover in Brian's colours was conveniently positioned at the bottom of a steep bank at Bluewaters pond that backed onto the yard, with a pump in it to lift water for washing the lorries. There was a hosepipe ban lasting many weeks and Brian could no longer put up with dirty lorries leaving the yard! The smart livery and clean appearance have for a long time been the hallmark of Brian Harris and now that the fleet has gone the roads are a duller place.

The 1970s saw a lot of change in the road haulage industry such as the first 40-foot trailers, the 32 ton gross weight limit, and at the end of the decade the introduction of the tachograph. Harris & Miners became Brian Harris. The workshops were extended to accommodate the new length trailers. The company was the first in Devon to have an 'A' Series ERF with the new 240 8-cylinder Gardner engine in 1973. Sid Knowles Transport in Penryn had the first in Cornwall at the same time. The colour scheme evolved into the format that lasted virtually unchanged until the end, and all the lorries carried names associated with Dartmoor. Drivers waited sometimes years to get on the firm and many stayed for decades. Brothers worked together (Derek and Jimmy Webster). Fathers and sons were drivers together (Bill and Billy Baty, Derek and Simon Webster, Dick and Brian Barrs, Tony and Alan Taylor). Drivers became fitters; it was very much a family thing. It was that sort of company that attracted considerable loyalty and many drivers who left often returned.

Brian had his own way of running the transport office which doubled as the tea-room, as apart from the workshops and store was the only covered space in the yard, unless you count the loo which had spent the last twenty years falling down and was barely covered at all! Talking of which, the cleaning of the loo was undertaken by Margaret Harris on Saturday mornings until the 1990s when Mick and Anne Whiteway took on the job. Mick was with the firm right at the beginning and still there at the end as part-time cleaner. The office was void of any modern technology except for a fax machine. All paper work was handwritten and much of the information needed to run such a business was carried in Brian's head. A one-man operated yard with a fleet covering the UK. If Brian ever (briefly) left the yard then operations virtually ceased as anyone delegated to answer the phone, which rang constantly, could only take a message. Other modern luxuries to make Brian's near forty years of running things more comfortable was his broken chair repaired with bits of pallets, and a single bar electric fire. If a driver were washing his lorry on the wash next to the office, then water would run through the wall and form a puddle at Brian's feet. If anyone remarked on this they were told in no uncertain terms that they had not been asked to sit in it!

As I have remarked, Brian Harris ran the business his way and no-one else would ever get near to helping, which made the operation unique. His way of pricing jobs was known only to him and largely made up on the day. Customers would often be charged a different rate for the same job on different days! A colleague of Brian's, Roger Eggbeer of Eggbeer's Transport in Newton Abbot, once told me an amusing anecdote when the two of them were together many years ago at the Royal Cornwall Hotel in Plymouth while attending a day's course concerning the CPC licence, which they both obtained by "Granny Rights". After being told various ways of calculating the mileage costs of running a lorry, all those attending (hauliers from all over the Southwest) were set a written question on pricing a load from A to B based on what they had just been told. Brian wrote nothing down but sat with his arms folded until the rest had written their answers on the paper in front of them. The lecturer could not help noticing this, so asked Brian for his answer, to which the reply came "£200". "Wrong Mr. Harris, it should be much more than that". "But I got the ----ing job, didn't I?" said Brian. And so it largely went on in that vein until March 2001. Wonderful.

So the method of operation was set and Brian has always said that if he was prevented from running the company his way, then he would close it down. A unique operation, which nevertheless gained a lot of respect throughout the industry. His name was so well known throughout the land that should a lorry break down then help was never far away. Drivers kept their own lorry, with its own ropes and sheets, and the artics seldom pulled any other trailer than the one supplied with it. They would then be tested annually as a pair. Every year the trailers were repainted, as were the chassis and wings of the units and rigids. The driver and his lorry would usually stick to the same run and often keep to the same customer, or customers. Loads were often transhipped from one trailer to another rather than change trailers. Quite often the only time a trailer was dropped was to grease the fifth wheel.

In 1977 whilst employed by Brian, I married Jenny and invited him to the wedding. He asked if we had organised a wedding car, as he would like to offer to do that himself with his new Jaguar. That appeared to be a condition of his accepting the invitation! My boss was my chauffeur on that day. He has always treated himself to a new Jaguar every three or four years, with very little mileage. (The last one had done only 7,000 and his fitter Reg did a fair proportion of that borrowing it for his holidays!). I have also borrowed a lorry for the last ten years from Brian to go to an annual vintage commercial vehicle run to carry the ex-Taunton Cider Leyland Octopus tanker that I am involved with, and on one such trip I had a puncture on the drive axle of the unit (Leyland Roadtrain) on a Sunday morning in Bournemouth. When you are borrowing someone else's gear that is just what you do not need. However, after one 'phone call to Brian he sorted it and got a firm to come out to us. I expect that job on a Sunday cost a few bob but Brian would not take a penny. When it came to settle up for the diesel we had used over the weekend I mentioned about the cost of the puncture, to which Brian replied, "what puncture?"

Gordon Bamsey beside his 8-wheel tipper which he had when new (1968). LUO 638F was the first 8-wheel tipper on the Harris & Miners fleet and the first 26 ton tipper built by ERF. (photo: Gordon Bamsey)

A publicity shot of the first 'A' series ERF with 240 Gardner sold by Frank Tucker Commercials of Exeter. The new twist lock (for containers) trailer has already been pressed into service carrying the flag poles for the stand at the 1972 Devon County Show. This lorry was registered YTT 675K and the name plate yet to be fitted on the front chassis would say 'Dartmoor Laddie'. Note the extra fog lights fitted beneath the bumper. (photo: David Corkery)

*DTA 279L 'Dartmoor Lassie' at the 1973 Devon County Show. The second ERF 'A' series to join the fleet.
(photo: David Corkery)*

*YFJ 495S out on the west coast of Scotland on a typical single track road. Miles of these roads had to be driven to get
to the places where the oil rigs were required. A regular trip for Brian Harris vehicles and drivers.
(photo: Brian Harris Collection)*

The last ERF 'A' series on the fleet. Bought new in 1975 without the sleeper pod and with Harris & Miners on the headboard. These alterations came in 1978 onwards as all the fleet were given Jennings conversions. RDV 686N 'Peter Davey' was photographed on the 24th September 1982 at Long Cliffe Quarries in Cornwall with 20 tons of English China Clay sheeted down but not yet roped. Presumably the driver is on a break or gone to fetch the tickets. (photo: Nigel Bunt)

A pair of ERF 'B' series loaded with pipes sit in the yard at Bovey Tracey in August 1983. The 240 straight 8 Gardner being the motive unit for these tractors. They were already 5 years old when this picture was taken but look new, including the trailers. Leaving the yard with a dirty outfit was also never an option. A crafty driver in a hurry might get away with just washing the offside of the vehicle as that was the side facing Brian's office as you drive out of the yard! (photo: Nigel Bunt)

A 1979 ERF with 240 straight 8 Gardner and 9-speed Fuller Roadranger Gearbox with a design gross weight of 38 tons sits at Trerulefoot in Cornwall on 27th June 1982 bearing the name of 'Uncle Tom Cobley'. (photo: Nigel Bunt)

"Dido" Brown gets in on the act again with his new lorry, 'Bill Brewer', at Roach on 26th June 1981. (photo: Nigel Bunt)

YFJ 495S 'Dartmoor Lassie' on the northbound M5 services at Michaelwood on a sunny June day in 1982. A clean and well presented outfit with a nicely sheeted load with the fly sheet, or top rider, over the ropes as is correct. (photo: Nigel Bunt)

Tom Pearce', Michaelwood Services July 1984. (photo: Nigel Bunt)

John Liddicoat with one drop left parked at Loch Leven in 1987. This unit had a 265 Gardner engine. There were three such units on the fleet: BTT, FTT and EOD. (photo: John Liddicoat)

'Dartmoor Lady', BTT 392Y, pictured southbound on Michaelwood services on 4th February 1983 when about 6 months old. This lorry was exhibited at the 1982 Royal Cornwall Show as UDV 739X but registered as 'Y' reg when put on the road a few months later. It was also the last lorry to be signwritten with Harris & Miners on the cab sides. (photo: Nigel Bunt)

'Dartmoor Roamer' sits next to a Spiers of Melksham AEC Mandator on the southbound Michaelwood Services in May1984. A 'C40' with 300 Turbo Gardner. When these cabs with the raised roofs first appeared they quickly got the nickname of dustcarts. This lorry had two bad accidents in its life on the fleet and Brian eventually sold it to Kings Potato Merchants of Collumpton for spares on the understanding it never went on the road again! (photo: Nigel Bunt)

B967 YTA 'Dartmoor Trooper' outside the Pottery Road depot in June 1990. Then driven by Warren 'Brummy' as can be seen written above the cab step. By the 1990s all the lorries had their driver's name signwritten on the off side. Many of them also had the names of wives or girlfriends written on the nearside. It all made work for the sign writer; especially when a lorry changed driver or a girlfriend was changed! (photo: David Henderson)

Chapter Six

THE AUTHOR REMINISCES. HIS DRIVING DAYS
WITH HARRIS & MINERS

(Note, this chapter was mainly compiled before the company closed in March 2001).

There can be few country pubs left untouched by the hand of modernisation. Few that have not become restaurants with a bar in the corner. Drinkers replaced by diners, where the Sunday roast now seems more popular in a country pub than at home. Well, I am glad to report that I know of just such a pub where the passage of time has left it largely unchanged and up to 1992 had changed but little in a generation. In fact, I doubt it changed at all. In August of that year Miss Audrey Lamb sold the Rugglestone Inn, on the edge of Widecombe-in-the-Moor, just a few yards from the home of Brian and Margaret Harris. The end of an era it definitely was, but luckily not the end of 'our' pub. Many incoming landlords fail to grasp that basic and all-important fact that the locals own the pub and in a small community change has to be done with care! Lorrie and Moira Ensor have been the proprietors ever since and while there has certainly been change it has happened in such a way that the character of the place remains intact. It is one of those gems we like to keep to ourselves in case too many people find out about it.

It was in the late 1960s that I first became aware of the Rugglestone Inn and Audrey was the landlady. There was no bar, just a serving hatch. No spirits, just beer and cider served straight from the barrel. Sherry and a small selection of wine, – one red, one white, – was kept as a concession to the ladies. There was no food except pickled eggs and crisps, and Audrey sold crisps only under sufferance, they generated crumbs you see. There was a "best" room but it was kept firmly under lock and key, and as I remember was only opened on Widecombe Fair day. The sign outside was extremely discreet with ivy covering most of it, which gave the impression that passing trade was actively discouraged. If you were not aware of it you could miss it and drive on by. There was no car park anyway. On entering its granite portals you would be very much aware of granite. Dartmoor granite. The whole building is constructed of it with a slate roof and flagstone floor. At the end of a short passageway was the serving hatch from where Audrey would serve the ale either straight from the barrel or from a large enamel jug. The choice was an excellent pint of draught Bass, or as above. For that was it except for a case of bottled beer kept for a very special local, Jerry Harris. To the right of the hatch was a room with a large oak table bounded by benches and an open fire in one corner. This was the second choice of where to sup one's ale, the other being in the passageway congregated around the serving hatch. Jerry had his own seat in the corner at the table and any unsuspecting passer-by not conversant with the house rules who inadvertently sat in Jerry's place would politely, but firmly, be told to move by Audrey. A tradition that Jerry started was a picture of his newest lorry pinned on the wall above his head. Each time a new lorry was bought the picture would change. More recently Mrs. Margaret Harris has continued the practice and the pictures are now framed.

Jerry would take his place in the "Ruggle" and hold court with a glass of White Shield Worthington in one hand and a Craven 'A' cigarette in the other. I can remember full bottles stacking up as those visitors who found the place kept buying, in return for his stories. Every time Audrey appeared with the jug to refill a holidaymaker's glass, she would say to them "and one for Jerry was it?" A wonderful arrangement between them.

It was here that I first met both Jerry and Brian and although by that time Brian was running the depot, Jerry was still the boss with Margaret very much in control of finances. Indeed, in spite of now being well into her eighties, Mrs. Harris still keeps a keen interest in, and involvement with the day-to-day running of the company. So, when I needed a job in 1975 as work with the timber haulage firm for whom I was driving an Atkinson slackened off, I was already known to them. An essential ingredient to being employed by Jerry and Brian was that they knew you. Even today a perfect stranger stands little chance of becoming a driver for Brian Harris and could be on a waiting list for years until he gets to know you. Even then the usual start is on a casual basis with the "getting on the books" something to aspire to at a later date. So, through drinking in the Rugglestone Inn I eventually was taken on as a driver by Brian in 1975. And what of the pub today? Well, that room never used in Audrey's day except on Widecombe Fair days is now a bar with a wider choice of ale but still from the barrel. How else? Spirits and food are also on sale now and a small car park has been carved out of the corner of the field opposite. It is still very much the Rugglestone Inn and remains a closely guarded secret.

The first lorry I drove for Harris & Miners (on a casual basis you understand) was OUO 340G; an AEC Mandator of 1969. There were two of these bought in 1969 with forty-foot trailers to go with them, the other was PDV 523G. A new unit was always bought with a trailer as they are invariably kept together as a pair throughout their working lives. One driver with his own unit and trailer, together with his own set of ropes and sheets. The way it has always been with Brian. It keeps the gear looking good as one man is responsible for it all and I liked working that way. Ken Simms was the regular driver of OUO and when I appeared as the new boy to drive his lorry while he was on holiday the ground rules were laid down by him in respect of which sheet did what and "don't you go ripping them". Two big sheets for paper, a clay sheet, and a flysheet plus half a dozen ropes hooked up behind the cab, and a sack full of scotches for reels of paper. Scotches? All right then, wedges. Three of us on that Monday morning went to load clay from Watts, Blake and Bearne at Kingsteignton. Tony Taylor with an 'A' Series ERF with a 240 Gardner, Ted Butt with the only Guy on the fleet, (Big J4T with Gardner 180), and me with the Mandator. All loaded with 20 tons apiece for Liverpool docks. All sheeted and roped and looking pretty (fly sheeted as well, of course), and it was back to the yard to wash down. Leaving on a trip without a clean lorry in the employment of Harris & Miners was never an option. "Got your bed booked?" was always the parting cry from Brian. A quick telephone call to the Shorthanger digs on the A38 north of Tewkesbury sorted that out and off we went in convoy.

Two and a half hours later the three of us pulled into the lorry park behind the digs. Always good food there and a pub, (The Crown), just across the road for the evening entertainment. That's another thing, drinking was definitely a qualification for joining Harris & Miners team in those days. A pub within walking distance of the digs was also a criterion of where we ended up at night. With an early start, Liverpool docks were reached by 9.00 a.m. I had got separated from the other two as the Mandator's silencer came loose on the M6 and I had a brief stop to tie it on as best I could. After unloading, it was "goodbye" to Ted and Tony as they had different jobs to do for the rest of the week. Apart from keeping your own lorry and trailer you normally had your own job to do as well. For years Ted, Tony, and Birdseye (Derek Webster) ran back into the yard together early on Sunday mornings, and as a rule, had Mondays off. The back shift as it was called. Ted "did the tyres" before that until he got a new lorry and I took on the Big J and "the tyres". Tony came back with Rayburns and paper and I will have to ask what Birdseye did. He is one of four men still on the firm since I left in 1978. His brother Jimmy Webster retired from Brian Harris three years ago and his son joined the company a few years ago. Derek is past retiring age and both Ted and Tony carried on well after their 65th birthdays. It's that sort of business. Not only run by a family, but several members of families drive for them. There have been, and still are, several examples of this happening. Bill Baty and his son Billy, both still on the scene. Dick Barrs and son Brian. Dick retired after driving the same lorry for twenty years! 'Old Faithful' as 373 FOD became affectionately known was pensioned off at the same time and now awaits restoration to show condition.

On leaving the docks I went to Trevor's of Warrington to pick up a load for Scotland, as there was a load of seed potatoes waiting for me at Ladybank, near Auchtermuchty in Fife, for my return load at the end of the week. Good digs at Kincardine Bridge, not far away. Trevor's ran a dozen or so Volvo F88s at that time and during my days with Harris & Miners I got to know them very well as the two companies worked together quite a bit. Now, that reminds me of an episode involving my dog. Skipper the Border Collie was a regular traveller with me in the cab and as a result I gained the nickname from Harris's drivers of "John the Dog"! Regular digs of ours in Scotland were at Blackwood, about twenty miles south of Glasgow, and we used to meet up with Trevors' drivers there. One of them, Jim, took a liking to my Skipper and said if we ever bred from him he would like one of the pups. Funny how events happen, for it was not long after this that the owners of a bitch Collie in Newton Abbot (where I was living at the time), approached me on that very subject. A deal was done and the two dogs introduced to each other at their superb house overlooking the sea at Dawlish. While me and Jenny (girlfriend then, wife now) sat around their swimming pool and drank their booze the dogs had the run of the garden to do what dogs do best. An excellent afternoon was had by all concerned! Jim requested that his pup should look just like Skipper, with the near perfect markings of a black and white Collie. So when the litter was born I picked the best looking one, as this was my part of the bargain. The bit I had not bargained for was getting a six-weeks old puppy to Warrington! I had my own lorry by then, which was the Big J Guy 'Peter Gurney'. Monday night at the Shorthanger digs was never the same again. The little bitch was quite the centre of attraction having travelled up from Devon with me. She was a little sweetie really and rarely stirred from her basket all the way to Warrington where she was duly delivered to Jim the next day as arranged. I believe £10 changed hands from a delighted new owner.

This was not the only time that Skipper had been in demand when I was "up the road". Normans of Ferrybridge were also digs I used when heading north on the A1. Skipper was usually with me and after an evening walk around the village, – every other house had a pigeon loft in that area it seemed, – we would end up in the Three Horseshoes for a pint. On one such visit I got talking to a sheep farmer who offered to buy Skipper to breed working Collies from. That was one deal I did not enter into. Skipper stayed with me until he died at 19 years of age.

After a few weeks of driving for Brian as a casual, and driving anything and everything, he offered me a full-time job and my own lorry. "You'd better come on the books then" was the way it was put and the lorry offered was a four-wheeler. JTA 505E, 'Moorland Princess' was an Albion with ergomatic cab, Leyland 401 engine, and twenty-two foot flatbed body. Multi-drops in Cornwall, which often included a night out at Redruth, were a regular job with this lorry, as was London and the south coast with paper and Candy tiles. Silvertown Motel on the Isle of Dogs became a regular haunt during my time with the Albion. On one such trip to London the engine started to sound distinctly unhealthy while running around the city with the usual load of bits and pieces. From one of the drops I rang Brian to tell him the bad news. He was anxious to get the lorry empty so asked if I could get the remaining drops off and see how it developed. "Go steady". Unfortunately I had to ring an hour later to say it had developed into a pool of oil on the road and things from within the engine trying to get out. That resulted in an engine rebuild at a garage Brian knew in the East End and a ride home for me in a W.F. Miners of Ashburton Volvo F88 driven by Geoff Woods from Chudleigh. Wherever you were in the country, and especially Scotland, help was never far away as Brian knows a lot of people and commands a lot of respect within the industry. When the Albion was fixed, a ride up with Brian Newbury got me back to London to finish the job a week later. Brian Newbury then drove a M.A.N. for Hottot Transport, also in Bovey Tracey, but is now driving a 7.5 tonner for Brian Harris. I did get to Scotland occasionally with the Albion and remember once bringing it back from Edinburgh with no clutch!

After a few months an artic was on offer as Ted Butt was getting the first 'B' Series ERF to join the fleet. His Big J Guy became mine. The 180 Gardner in that lorry was the smoothest Gardner I have known. It was coupled to a six-speed Thornycroft 'box and a York trailer. The entire outfit weighed less than 11 tons and at a plated gross weight maximum in those days of 32 tons it would legally carry 21.5 tons. Not bad for a 180 when you think that today's lorries have more power than that in a four-wheeler, although they do go up hills a bit quicker! It had no power steering, which made me sweat a bit when fully freighted in small space. The heater only worked efficiently when the engine was under load, which meant running up the M5 and M6 to Scotland was a cold affair, other than on the banks such as Beattock. The radio was an afterthought screwed to the back of the cab and it had no sleeper cab. None did while Jerry was alive. In those days there were plenty of transport digs available and he maintained you were fit for nothing the next day if you had to spend the night in the cab. How times have changed. With its outdated features, (remember this lorry was built at the same time that Scania was offering the 110 and Volvo the F88), I loved it. After all, I knew no better, up until then I had only known British trucks apart from the odd lift, and I was now an artic driver on the Harris & Miners fleet.

However, it was not long before I did get a taste of a foreign lorry. One of the contracts Harris & Miners had was for Geest Bananas. A trunk from Spalding to their depot at Heathfield, Newton Abbot, and shared with Gill's Transport of Chudleigh. I did the last couple of runs before the contract ended and Geest put their own motors on it. My Big J developed a brake problem in Spalding so Geest lent me one of their tractor units to pull my trailer. They arranged to repair the brakes overnight in their own workshops and the next load would be brought down by a Geest driver and my unit with one of their trailers. And what did they lend me? A Volvo! No disrespect to the good old British Guy, and I know Brian reckoned it was a good buy, but from a driver's point of view you just had to prefer the Volvo. It had a sprung seat for a start. I am sure a life's back trouble started with that Big J's driving position and seat bolted firmly to the back of the cab. When the Geest driver turned up at Heathfield with it to swap over he couldn't get back into his Volvo quickly enough and I was reluctant to get out of it. His parting comment was "how the hell do you drive that?" Nevertheless, the British lorry holds a great deal of my affection and they were good days to have been around in as a driver.

Another regular load that Harris & Miners had were Dunlop tyres from Inchinnon, on the northern outskirts of Glasgow, to the Dunlop depot in Southampton and the Ford Transit factory, also in Southampton. I took on this run and kept it until leaving the company. The tyres were always picked up on a Wednesday for delivery on Friday. Union rules demanded that I had a second man to help load. Willie was that man who lived at Blackwood and I picked him up every Wednesday morning at 7.00 a.m. to get us to the tyre factory by 8.00 a.m. A full load was a mixture of all sizes from wheelbarrow tyres to tractor tyres and was about 1,300 in total, all on a flat trailer. They came down a chute and Willie rolled them up the trailer to me one by one. By the time they were stacked, sheeted and roped, it was the middle of the afternoon and back to Blackwood for the night. Pay Willie for his days work, get cleaned up and changed and over to the café for a meal before spending the evening in Dougie's Bar. Harris & Miners' drivers had their own room at those digs; such was the regularity of our trips to Scotland. Thursday was a day at the wheel heading south so as to be in Southampton for 8.00 a.m. on Friday. Ring Brian when tipped to see if there was anything in the area to pick up and head for home. As often as not there would be 20 tons of bagged clay from E.C.C. at Wareham for me which could be my load to Scotland on Monday. Dragging that lot back to Devon up Charmouth and Chideock was probably the hardest part of the week, especially with a Gardner 180!

In 1976 Billy Baty joined the firm and drove an ERF four-wheeler for a time before he too was given an artic. He is one of the few men from my days who are still employed by Brian. He is in the workshops now with Reg Hill, who was also a colleague of mine in the '70s. Brian picked up a job of five loads to Southern Ireland, which was for a drop-sided four-wheeler. Brick fireplaces it was from Brock's Fireplaces of Kingsbridge. Billy was not particularly impressed with going to the Irish Republic as he had just left the Royal Navy and had seen enough of Ireland. HTA 742D, with Gardner 120, David Brown gearbox, and Eaton two-speed axle became mine for those trips as the two of us swapped lorries. My grandmother on my father's side of the family had owned a pub in Dublin and I have Irish blood in me, so I volunteered myself for the task. Somebody had to do it.

Fleetwood to Dublin on a roll-on roll-off ferry for lorries called the Buffalo was the crossing booked for all five trips and the destination in Southern Ireland was a brick works in Athy, on the way to Limerick. I hope the country has not changed too much since I was last there twenty-five years ago, as the whole place was so laid back and the people so friendly. There were many incidents still so fresh in my mind that just could not have happened anywhere else. Those five loads spread over six months and covered both winter and summer. On one winter trip I left the docks in Dublin at 4.00 a.m. with my usual 10 tons of fireplaces and on the outskirts of the city skidded all over the road on ice. I eventually came to a halt at the side of the road and enquired of a passing police car, The Garda, as to why the roads were not gritted, only to be told that it was too cold and a bit early to be sending the gritters out! On a summer trip I got to my destination to be told by the owner of the brick works that it was Dublin races that day and everyone was going. I was taken to the races by the boss and a good day was had by all. The next day I got unloaded and headed back to Dublin for the midnight ferry back to Fleetwood. As I had time to spare, – there was only one sailing per day, – I decided to find what had been my grandmother's pub some years before. The Swan Bar, Cork Street, Dublin. I was eventually re-united with my lorry on the docks just in time to board the ferry after a session on the Guinness with some locals of the Swan Bar. Perhaps it was not such a good idea to tell them about me granny!

In those days there was no MOT in Southern Ireland, nor did it seem that gross weight counted for much either. On one of my trips to the brick works Brian organised a back load of drainage castings from Athy to somewhere in Lancashire. They loaded ten crates on the bed of the lorry, (the 10 ton four-wheel ERF), and then started putting another row on top which looked awful heavy to me! On enquiring I found that the crates were a ton apiece and they were quite happy to let me have twenty of them. Not on my lorry thank you! I left with 10 tons, which seemed to completely baffle the Irish; as to them I only had half a load. On another visit to Athy a Mandator artic of local extraction, that was falling to bits but had just travelled miles across Ireland, followed me into the brick works. It did not even have any mirrors and on talking to its very Irish driver he informed me that mirrors were of no importance to him as he wasn't interested in where he had been! Wonderful way to carry on if you can get away with it, and they certainly did then.

Another lovely little incident while across the Irish Sea involved an Irish docker and a flat battery. There I was sitting in a pub on Ferry Road in Dublin with my lorry outside waiting to go down to the docks for the midnight ferry back to Blighty. When I came to leave, HTA 742D would not start because I had left the sidelights on as I was parked on the street. Well, at the time it seemed the right thing to do! If I missed the ferry I would miss my pick up the next morning, which was the ring mat from the Blackpool Tower Circus. This I had to take somewhere in Devon to have done to it whatever circus ring mats need doing to them after years of being trampled on by elephants. Anyway, all I could think of was a means to start my lorry, so I ran the mile or so (I was fitter then) to the docks to see if I could get help. I found an Irish docker in charge of a Tugmaster manoeuvring artic trailers onto the ferry I was supposed to be catching. Armed with a length of chain he was only too pleased to abandon what he was doing and head off down Ferry Road with me, and his unlit tug, to give my lorry a snatch start. I made the ferry with minutes to spare and I shall be eternally grateful to the docker whose name I never found out and who refused any kind of tip. That was one of those events that stick in my mind because it was so alien to the reception I was used to at some of the docks in this country. Well, most of the docks in this country actually, as any driver of my   generation, and who had the job of going into docks in the '70s will know what I am saying. The days of union power and weak management that between them finished off a lot of our industry and closed most of the docks. Remember picket lines and "Red Robbo" who almost single-handedly decimated British Leyland? It all seems a long time ago now but the lorry driver had a lot to put up with at that time. I remember going into East Canada dock, Liverpool, with the Guy Big J and empty trailer for 20 tons of Argentinean corned beef. As I had no pallets to give in return my load had to be handballed off the pallets on which it had just crossed the Atlantic and re-stacked onto the bed of my trailer. Farcical isn't it? The whole idea of pallets is to minimise constant handling of the goods. A fact that passed over the 1970s Liverpool docker, which meant that half an hour job was turned into four hours hard graft. Oh, and that's not all. The forklift driver would only bring the bloody corned beef to the rear of the trailer so I had to carry each carton of tins the full length of my trailer and stack them on my own. After it was all roped and sheeted the forklift driver must have had a tinge of compassion for me as he gave me a case of the stuff all for myself. Then it dawned on me, all he had done was give me some of the corned beef he had pinched in the first place! On a recent visit to Liverpool I could not help but notice the almost complete absence of shipping on the Mersey and the brown heritage signs indicating where the docks used to be. Now there's a surprise.

Hull docks did not fare much better either, especially King George V dock. Brian sent me in there with a sample package of clay to be put on a ship for Dar es Salaam, Tanzania. I was then driving DTA 279L, the 'A' Series ERF, and pulled into the docks with an empty flat trailer and the sample bag of clay on the floor of the cab. In front of me were twenty or so loaded lorries queuing for the same ship, so I walked my bag of clay under my arm to the front of the queue to find the office and someone in charge. Makes sense so far, doesn't it? Obviously this was too much for the someone in charge as I was told to wait my turn behind the twenty or so 20 ton loads. A days wait for one small package of Watts, Blake and Bearne's very finest plastic clay to be accepted and signed for. I did not think so. I left it with the notes at the foot of the someone in charge and was gone within half an hour with the words of "you're blacked" ringing in my ears. Brian never sent me to Hull docks again.

Although my time driving for Harris & Miners in the '70s were possibly not the best days of labour relations, and bloody-minded working practices were something we came up against on almost every trip, they were, nevertheless, good days to have been part of the road haulage scene. The traffic was a fraction of what it is today. I could leave Devon for Scotland on any day, at any time, and know to within minutes what time I would get to Penrith or Blackwood. Winter weather was practically the only cause for delay. I remember being north of Aberdeen with diesel frozen to a jelly state in a blizzard once thinking, "what the hell am I doing this for?" Today the same journey will almost certainly involve traffic jams on the M5 or M6 somewhere. One such delay comes to mind which involved nobody else but me. It would have been 1975 and I was driving OOD 504M, which was usually in the hands of Maurice Gouldthorpe. It was one of five, straight eight 240 Gardner engined 'A' Series ERFs on the fleet and one I had for a couple of weeks while Maurice was away, (he is sadly no longer with us). As I was not totally familiar with this lorry I was not aware of its completely, hopelessly inaccurate fuel gauge, and spluttered to a halt on the A38 at Beam Bridge, just west of Wellington in Somerset, with a trailer load of straw. The M5 had not yet reached these parts. This lorry had two diesel tanks, as all the artics had, which were supposed to drain equally and the gauge read off one of them. Unfortunately everyone else except me, (perhaps as the new boy this was some kind of initiation), knew that it ran out of one tank faster than the other. The feed to the engine was from the side that ran down the quickest and the gauge on the dashboard was connected to the other tank. I still had plenty of diesel, but in the wrong tank. Remedy, dog's bowl used as a container to tranship enough fuel from the nearside tank to the offside one to get me to the garage at the top of the hill and fill up. That garage, like so many on the old trunk roads ceased fuel sales years ago.

Tachographs and mobile 'phones were not thought of. CB radio was very much a new toy and initially on the illegal AM band, which meant jobsworths would lurk about on motorway service stations to confiscate the sets from drivers. I never had a sleeper cab the whole time I drove for Harris & Miners. I used to "cab it" with a piece of board from the engine cover to the window ledge to sleep on when on straw in the summer months, but it was generally frowned upon by Jerry Harris, whose parting words as you left the yard were always "have you got your bed booked, son?" Brian would tell you to "ring me when you're tipped". Many older drivers will remember the Red Book listing all the transport digs up and down the country. Kempsey, Brock, Blackwood, The Hollies, Penkridge, The Albion at Penrith, and Carlisle Truck Stop to name but a few of them, and all never very far from a pub. Some of these digs were frequented by Harris & Miners' drivers so often that we had our own room!

During my time with the company I witnessed the Motorway network from the Southwest to Scotland gradually all link up. I remember Ted Butt proudly boasting late in 1975 that he had just driven for the first time from the Scottish border to Exeter on a motorway all the way. Life on the road would never be the same again.

The Ergomatic cabbed Albion driven by the author in 1975 appearing in Chudleigh Carnival in the summer of that year. The youngsters on the back were from a sort of reform school near Chudleigh (now closed) and were a little difficult to control. The theme for this float was from a topical television programme of the day 'It Aint Half Hot Mum' which meant having the school piano on the lorry. The author remembers as he was driving in the carnival the kids chucking the piano off the back of the lorry! Perhaps this is where the expression 'fell off the back of a lorry' started!' Anyway, it disintegrated into a thousand pieces. (photo: author)

DTA 279L, 'Dartmoor Lassie', at Leith Docks on 14/8/1974 when driven by Reg Hill. As we get into the 1970s the livery starts to get a little more fancy as can be seen here with the telephone number in a decorative ring. DTA 279L can always be identified from the other 3 'A' series artics as it has a dark background to the headboard. (photo: J. Donaldson)

XOD 118S 'Dartmoor Laddie'. Pictured 30/4/84. Southbound Taunton Deane M5 services. The name was taken from the first 'A' series (YTT 675K) which this lorry replaced. During the transitional period from Harris & Miners to Brian Harris Transport Limited new lorries were still liveried as Harris & Miners with a Brian Harris headboard. This cab is fitted with a Jennings sleeper conversion which affords considerably more room for the driver of the 'B' series ERF than its predecessor. By the look of the sheets this is another multi-drop load in which Brian specialised. A good pay-load as they say! (photo: Nigel Bunt)

Brian bought 3 ERF 'B' series 6 wheel flatbeds second-hand at the end of the 1970s. KSC 97N is a very early example of the 'B' series seen here at Roach Cafe on 7th Feb. 1983. It is a 6x4 with 27 foot body, model 25G-3RD-DB4, chassis no 029977. (photo: Nigel Bunt)

Only a year or so old when pictured on 3rd November 1981 at Roach. The black bumper suggests an earlier altercation with something or other. The Captain Birdseye in the windscreen was the nickname of the driver, Derek Webster. Note the spelling of the name, 'Dan'l Whiddon'. (photo: Nigel Bunt)

REH 186R, 'Dartmoor Princess', pictured in the Bovey Tracey yard 27/11/82. This is a 6x4 with 25 foot flatbed. All three ERF 6-wheelers were powered by Gardner 180s and designed for 25 ton gross weight. (photo: Nigel Bunt)

'Bill Brewer' and Dido Brown loading clay at Long Cliffe, Cornwall, 26/11/82. (photo: Nigel Bunt)

XTA 444S 'Tom Pearce' spotted on 9th March 1983 when 5 years old. Gordano Services looks to be the location and Scottish seed potatoes on their way to Cornwall a likely looking load. Note the dunnage carried between the trailer legs. (photo: Nigel Bunt)

A Leyland Steer of early fifties vintage with Bill Baty (senior) the proud driver. This lorry then passed on to Alf Harvey and Gordon Bamsey before being sold to the Westcountry showmen, T. Whitelegg and Sons. This was a twin-steer 6-wheeler with the handbrake actuating on the second steer axle. It had a Leyland 600 engine of 9.8 litres and 5 speed gearbox. 782 BTA caught fire three times during its life with the fairground! A relative of the Whitelegg family was present at the auction on April 18th 2001. (photo: Brian Harris Collection)

373 FOD 'Happy Wanderer' photographed in Bodmin in May 1979 when nearly 20 years old and still working. Dick Barrs took this lorry on when new in 1960 and kept it until he retired 20 years later. Chassis number 009606, model number KV54G2, 14 tons gross. Powered by a Gardner 5LW and with 20 foot Boalloy body. It also has a Boalloy cab. (photo: Nigel Bunt)

An aerial view of the Bovey Tracey depot in 1968. This former pottery site had been acquired by Harris & Miners in 1957. Underneath the main building is a water wheel which although unseen for many years is still there. The ramp was a recent addition to comply with the recently introduced plating and testing regulations for heavy goods vehicles. The new workshops and store, which were built to the right of the ramp, did not materialise until 1970. There were no doors on this shed until 1962! Brian's office is the little annex with the whitewashed wall and remains as such to the present day; he is still in attendance every day. The woodland to the right and left is now developed with housing as is the allotment in the bottom left corner. It can clearly be seen that the company was on that site long before the new houses were built but it still did not stop the new residents from complaining about living next to a transport yard. (photo: Brian Harris Collection)

HTA 742D in the yard in 1976. 'Devon Pixie' was powered by a 6LW Gardner and had an air operated two-speed axle. It was an LV64G with triple dropside aluminium body with a payload of 10 tons. It caught fire early in its life which destroyed the top of the cab and when finally taken out of service someone pinched most of the engine! It was already 10 years old when this picture was taken and was the lorry the author took to the Republic of Ireland on 5 trips in 1976 and 1977. (photo: Author)

JTA 505E, 'Moorland Princess', brings many memories back to the author as he drove it on a regular basis before being offered an artic. This 1967 Albion with Leyland 401 engine and 22 foot flat had a payload of 10 tons. Before John was its driver it was rolled into a ditch at Bean Bridge on the Devon and Somerset border and was re-cabbed. Exceptionally clean for a 10 year old lorry. John's creature comforts can be seen in the cab; blanket over the engine cover; smart gear hanging up on the passengers side and girly calendar behind the drivers seat! (photo: Author)

Tommy Edwards and second man as required by Dunlop to load the tyres at Inchinnon; with 'Dartmoor Lady' on Ballieston Street in Glasgow on the 19th April 1972. LUO 287F is a 1968 example of a Leyland Super Comet. (photo: John Henderson)

A winters day, January 1976, at the Harris & Miners yard in Bovey Tracey. On such mornings Alf Harvey would often have the task of pushing a wheelbarrow with batteries and jump leads from lorry to lorry to get them started with the resultant clouds of white smoke as the Gardner engines spluttered into life. Here are two Gardner engined ERFs and a V8 Cummins engined 'D' series Ford driven by Norman Crowe on Scottish distance work. In those days mileage meant money and it paid well to send 4-wheelers with multi-drops to Scotland. However, in more recent times mileage meant high costs with the excessive fuel tax levied by stupid politicians.

Note the chrome ringed radio pod and speaker at the back of the cab of the 8-wheeler. LUO 638F, 'Widecombe Lad', was very much a distance motor and a far cry from the luxuries and sound systems of todays vehicles. This drop-sided tipper was new to the fleet in 1967 and was powered by a Gardner 180 with 6-speed David Brown (round the corner 4th. to 5th) gearbox. (photo: Author)

LUO 638F in the Bovey Tracey depot in 1968. The sign writing was done in gold leaf on this lorry, behind which can be seen a Commer and a couple of Leylands that were on the fleet in those days. (photo: Gordon Bamsey)

Billy Baty with a sleeper cab addition on YTT, 'Dartmoor Laddie'. His load of Powrmatic heaters have made a bit of a mess of the sheet! These Jennings conversions started appearing on the ERF 'A' series in 1978. The Michelin Man was very much the thing to have in those days! (photo: Bill Baty)

OOD 504M, 'Dartmoor Lady', loaded with clay for Scotland in 1974. Maurice "Silent" Gouldthorpe had this 'A' series when new. Powered by a Garner 240 straight eight. (photo: Brian Harris Collection)

'Moorland Queen' has the East Anglian registration of MDO 855P and is a 6x2 configuration with 27 foot body. Michaelwood services on 26th June 1982, southbound. (photo: Nigel Bunt)

January 1976 sees an ERF 'A' series with Gardner 240 sitting in the yard with its trailer loaded with waste paper for Muggy Moss, Aberdeen. Derek 'Birdseye' Webster obviously felt little benefit from the heater by the way he has blanked off the radiator. (photo: Author)

'Widecombe Lad', southbound M5 services at Michaelwood on 14/6/82. 'Greedy boards' are in use to get the maximum weight of coal on, probably 20 tons. An 8-wheel tipper on distance work is a rare sight today. (photo: Nigel Bunt)

'Dartmoor Lady' on the Wincanton stand of the Royal Cornwall Show on 12th June 1982. Chassis number 046605 was powered by an 8LXC Gardner 8-cylinder 249 bhp engine with a design gross weight of 40 tons. Fitted with twin stainless steel tanks and Autolube automatic chassis lubrication system. UDV 739X never went on the road bearing that registration but went on the road later that year as BTT 329Y. The dealer jumped the gun a bit by registering the vehicle when Brian did not want it on the fleet until it replaced one being taken off the road. (photo: Nigel Bunt)

The 'Old Grey Mare' waits patiently for the driver on Michaelwood Services (northbound) in February 1984. (photo: Nigel Bunt)

The ex-Reeve and Grossart ERF repainted in Brian's livery but retaining the light blue and thistle emblem on the cab sides. KSU 762V is now named 'Widecombe Warrior' seen here at Roach Cafe in March 1984. (photo: Nigel Bunt)

Peter Davey at Roach Cafe in June 1984. A 'C38' Gardner 265 motor. (photo: Nigel Bunt)

'Dartmoor Lady' under the first tri-axle trailer on the fleet which was converted from a tandem axle by Heavy Transport of Plympton. This C40 ERF was powered by a 265 Gardner and driven by Reg Hill. (photo: Brian Harris Collection)

Pat McKenna in the yard with part of a drilling rig from Seacore at Gweek, near Helston, which was destined for the north west of Scotland. (photo: Brian Harris Collection)

The first Leyland Roadtrain on the fleet with neatly flysheeted load. 'Peter Gurney' was supplied with a 320 Cummins engine and 9-speed Fuller Roadranger gearbox. (photo: Nigel Bunt)

B71 WDV was new in 1984. John C took this photograph to add to his portfolio to show off his sign writing skills. The entire vehicle was hand written by John and represents four and a half days work. (photo: Author)

'Peter Gurney' was the first of two Leyland Roadtrains to be bought by Brian and is seen here loaded with Dartmoor granite for Aberdeen. (photo: Brian Harris Collection)

'Dartmoor Trooper' in July 1989 on Michaelwood Services (southbound). (photo: Nigel Bunt)

Warren Piggot drove YTA in the early 1990s and affectionally named it 'The Old Lady' as it was then the oldest motor on the fleet. A38 Man? That's where he went all the time. (photo: Dave Brewer)

A smartly presented 'Peter Gurney' and matching curtainsided loaded with tyres. This lorry was converted from Gardner to Cummins after the original engine seized up. (photo: Brian Harris Collection)

A 1985 tractor bought second hand. Bill Brewer was powered by a Cummins 320 Turbo. The Gardner engine was now no longer specified and the fleet soon changed from an ERF Gardner engined one to a largely Cummins engined operation. It proved extremely reliable and capable of mileages previously unheard of. (photo: Nigel Bunt)

This brightly painted little Roadrunner was for Derek "Soapy" Hudson to drive after a heart attack deprived him of his H.G.V. licence and he had to come off the arctics. 'Dartmoor Firefly' is loaded with a bin from T.T.B. of Dartmouth. (photo: Brian Harris Collection)

The 'Old Grey Mare' at the Hollies in April 1989. B149 ATT is behind. Colin was the driver at this part of the lorry's existence. He left the company to pursue a driving career in the USA. (photo: Nigel Bunt)

Richard Basson at the wheel of one of the two Seddon Atkinsons that were on the fleet. Photographed near Derby in 1995. (photo: Brian Harris Collection)

Graham 'Swivel' Perkins climbing on to the back of the Leyland Brian bought second-hand from George Coker of Ivybridge. 'Widecombe Lady' is being loaded with cattle feed at D. Brimmacombe of Crediton. (photo: Brian Harris Collection)

Sam Proctor was the final driver of this lorry before closure. 'Phantom of the Moor' is here loaded with coal at Broughton Doncaster, for Torquay. (photo: Brian Harris Collection)

F105 ORG loaded with a grain dryer from Yate destined for Scotland. A rear-steer unit fitted with a crane. (photo: Brian Harris Collection)

A lovely night time photograph under the lights of a motorway services. (photo: Brian Harris Collection)

By 1977 the author was driving this ERF 'A' series with Gardner 240 and had the permission from Brian Harris to use it privately to take 3 vintage tractors, belonging to friends Brian Beard and Nat Clifford, to the Great Working of Steam Engines in Dorset on September 24th. and 25th. It was a muddy one that year and the lorry's name plate has been removed to reveal the chassis as to get up to, or away from, the loading ramp a tow by tractor was essential. There were 192 of them entered that year! DTA 279L 'Dartmoor Lassie' was new in 1973 and its first driver was Reg Hill. John took it on in 1977 and remained his lorry until he left the company for a career change a year later. (photo: Author)

Bert Long with 'Dartmoor Lady' taking a boat from Great Yarmouth to Howard Marine in Plymouth. (photo: Brian Harris Collection)

Graham Perkins and his ERF eight-wheeler 'Happy Wanderer'. (photo: Brian Harris Collection)

Peter Rees drove the only Leyland Daf ever to appear on the fleet. (photo: Brian Harris Collection)

'Dartmoor Lassie' being loaded in the yard on the 17th. of March 2001, less than two weeks before the closure was announced by Brian. This unit is now owned by Parsons Transport of Aylesbeare and is at present pulling for Fine Tubes of Plymouth; a contract taken over from Brian Harris. Stan did this job for Brian and was taken on by Parsons to do the same run. Although this is a different unit to the one Stan drove for Brian it remains in Brian's colours and he is pulling the trailer he had when working for Brian. (photo: Nigel Bunt)

The first Sunday in September at the start of the 1992 Bournemouth to Bath Run for historic commercial vehicles, Kings Park, Boscombe. The author, John, and friends have now been taking this 1949 Leyland Octopus, once operated by Taunton Cider, to road runs and shows up and down the country with the kind generosity of Brian Harris by lending the means of carrying the 8-wheeler to the start of the event. This well-presented Leyland Road Train proved ideal for the job and John could play with an artic from time to time! 'Moorland Princess' was normally driven by Billy Baty (Bosun Bill) and pulled a Tautliner; hence the roof spoiler. (photo: Author)

The prototype Corgi model sent to the author (who was dealing with the project) for approval. (photo: Paul Lapsley Photography)

Barrier down and shut down as the lorries come home and get parked up after 6th. April 2001. (photo: Author)

Reg Hill and Gordon Bamsey making ready for the auction. (photo: Author)

The fleet being lined up for the forthcoming auction. A magnificent fleet of traditional liveried ERFs about to go under the hammer and never to be seen together again. (photo: Author)

Kenny Myson drove this rig when new and always kept an immaculate outfit. Note the super singles on the steer axle. Phil Hoskin in the red jumper looks on. He is joint proprietor (with his wife) of Parsons Transport, Exeter, and is a good friend of Brian. The tractor made £12,000 and the trailer £11,600. (photo: Author)

Lot 168 made £250. Brian's lorry before he took over the office. It was parked up when 3 years old! 932 MDV was new in 1963 for Brian to drive at the age of 21. This 7 ton Thames Trader was in the regular habit of carrying considerably more than its design weight so a reliable source informs the author! A previous Trader (363 GTT) had been especially built under 3 tons unladen so Brian could drive it when aged only 17. (photo: Author)

Brian Harris emerges from his office after the final lot falls under the hammer. The lorry behind him made £7,000 (lot 154). (photo: Author)

Chapter Seven

MEMORIES AWAKENED. DRIVERS' TALES FROM 1946

All the drivers I have spoken to since writing this book have very fond memories of the company they once worked for. I will also include myself as one with such memories as, of course, I am also an ex-driver of Harris & Miners. Drivers came and went, as they do in any company, but there was always that happy atmosphere like one big family with this very special company. Many stayed for decades; some left and returned a few years later, and at least three sons joined their fathers as drivers. Even after it has all finished and closed down we are in touch with each other and hear what everyone is now doing through the jungle telegraph. There has been a reunion get-together that included Brian. My task of writing this story had been made a pleasure as ex-employees were happy to tell some of their experiences, (many unprintable), and give me telephone numbers of someone else with another bit of information.

One Saturday two old mates rang me eager to relate what they could remember of their time with either Harris & Miners, or Brian Harris, or both. Bert Long rang to ask when the book was coming out and that he wanted three copies. He started in 1960, a few months after Ted Butt. He drove one of two early fifties Albions on the fleet with coach built wooden framed cabs. His was VDV 241, which was a six-wheeler Reiver with 4-cylinder Albion oil engine of 93 b.h.p. It was "as flat as a strap" he recalls, and needed crawler gear to get up Lamb Hill towards Morgan's Café on the A38. The other Albion was an artic driven by Alan Tapper and is buried somewhere under the toilets! Bert left in 1964 to join W.F. Miners but returned for a few more years in the 1980s. Shortly after that conversation Peter Rees rang and said he wanted four copies. When Brian Harris closed Peter was then the driver with the longest number of years unbroken service. He started with Harris & Miners in January 1966 having given up a career in the police. Thirty-five years later he was there at the end, although it nearly ended in tears on his third day. He ended up in a ditch in Botley, near Southampton, and wrote off the AEC Mercury he was driving. It transpired the accident was caused by mechanical failure – a wheel bearing seized, – so it was not his fault. I have been "up the road" with Peter when he was driving a Dodge and I had an Albion, and we have been in a pub together where there was a piano. You hum it and Peter can play it. It's a gift.

Another little story to emerge from several old hands, (I got it first from Ted Butt and when Ted is in full flight you have to listen), was about one of the Commer artics. 'Jimpy' as it became known was the petrol engined one of the two. ROD 881 was converted from an artic unit and had a flat body built on it, which Brian had to learn to drive on when he was 17. It was his first lorry and it ended its days doing local collections and deliveries, giving Brian a step in the right direction before going on long distance with his first Thames Trader. Many of the older drivers remember Brian as a lad going with them to quite literally "learn the ropes". There was no privilege and he started at the bottom doing the job himself.

Mick Whiteway was with the company almost from the start and in his driving days recalls being done for speeding twice on the same trip in 1955 driving an AEC through Slough. He was only going at the speed of the rest of the traffic, but his lorry was restricted to 20 m.p.h. (a 20 miler as they were known) and he was clocked at 28 m.p.h. On the return journey he drove all the way out of London and through Slough at 18 m.p.h. causing chaos to the traffic. He yet again got pulled over by a policeman for causing an almighty tailback! 18 m.p.h., however, at just 2 m.p.h. below the legal limit for lorries over 3 tons unladen was perfectly legal. Eventually after many protests and convoys of lorries doing 18 m.p.h. through busy conurbations the speed limit was raised to 30 m.p.h.

The picture of Mick and Ann camping in a farmer's field with the Commer artic unit with them shows a happy young couple enjoying a trip to Scotland and getting paid for doing it. However, the return journey was marred by the incredible attitude of a particular café proprietor. Mick and Ann pulled into a transport café on the A74 between Lockerbie and Gretna to be told by the woman behind the counter that she did not serve drivers with women. She did not serve sluts! The fact that Mick told her Ann was his wife cut no ice, so they left with the passing words from Ann that she hoped the place burnt down. Two weeks later it did. To put the record straight Ann felt guilty of her comments at the time and assures me the fire had no connection with her!

On another trip Mick was driving the Commer with P6 Perkins when the starter motor became detached from the bell housing at Duro's Café in Stoke-on-Trent. Duro's was a favourite haunt for drivers in the '50s and '60s, having large dormitories sleeping fifty or so drivers in the pre-sleeper cab days. He drove to the Commer factory at Wolverhampton who sent him on his way with a temporary repair. The following week Jerry asked him to go away with that lorry with no starter at all. He did the East Coast run to East Anglia with no starter. A week away with either the engine running, or parked on a slope! Do not for one moment think that this action puts a cloud on the maintenance or operation of Harris & Miners, but things were very different fifty years ago. Mick got sacked one day for some discrepancy on a weighbridge and reinstated on the next when an urgent load had to go. Such was the way of things in those days.

Mick became an invaluable part of the team as years went on with many exploits up and down the country as a fitter. He and Alf Harvey, who joined him in the workshop, did an incredible job keeping the fleet moving during their years as fitters. Brian Harris would send them all over the land to fix a stricken lorry and parts would be loaded into Brian's 3 litre Capri to rush off to some problem. Brian had a string of high performance Fords which were often seen tearing up some motorway or other loaded with tools and a diff, or whatever, to sort out a stranded lorry. Mick rebuilt an engine on the lorry park at Blackwood, south of Glasgow, and changed a spring on a Dodge at the same place. He rebuilt a failed turbo on Heston Services for Peter Rees' Dodge, and attended to Dido Brown in 1986 on the A406 North Circular Road with missing wheels off his trailer! That was a three hours dash from Bovey Tracey in Brian's 2.8 injection Sierra loaded with a new hub for the repair. The policy was that a fast response from Bovey Tracey was infinitely better than a call-out from some commercial repairers in the area. With a fast car and a willing fitter it usually worked, as long as Brian wasn't too fussy about his car! In later years his Jaguar was pushed into similar service.

Bill Baty joined the company in 1946 at the age of 19 and recalls an episode resulting in a burnt out lorry. It was a Ford petrol engined V8 and it happened in 1948. There were three of them in the cab returning to the Widecombe depot when the lorry developed a blockage in the carburettor jet, so with the engine cover removed inside the cab the one in the middle was pouring petrol from a can directly into the carb. Suddenly the engine spat back with a flame, resulting in the petrol can being thrown up in the air with the obvious disastrous outcome. The three of them did manage to escape the inferno but Jerry was not best pleased. If things were going well Jerry would refer to you as "my son", but if you were addressed as "mister" then expect the worst. "Mister" was the term used on that day.

Bill also took Brian with him on Scottish runs when he was a lad. Brian's job was to look out for the speed cops and keep an eye on the road behind. Bill remembers driving the Leyland Steer which he had from new. This would have been sometime in the late '50s and Brian identified a following police car. They were doing about 32 m.p.h. which was almost a hanging offence in those days, but the copper said he had not stopped them for that, but had identified the lorry as being from Devon, and he and the wife were going on holiday to Devon in a couple of weeks and wanted to find out where to go and what to see. Although Bill's old red book licence is littered with speeding endorsements from those days he was let off on that occasion.

Jerry had a customer in Plymouth called Fine Tubes (who remained customers until closure) and one of the managers had an elderly aunt who had died in Plymouth while on a visit from Scotland. Could Jerry help in getting the body back to Scotland? After negotiations it was agreed that Mick and Bill should do the job, using the Land Rover with the company at the time. The coffin was loaded in the back and off they went, stopping at a transport café near Stafford on the way. On leaving they were asked for a lift from a hitchhiker wanting to get to Scotland. Mick and Bill were a bit unsure because of their unusual load in the back. However, it was dark and the young chap was almost pleading to be taken, so they said he could sit in the back, under the canvas tilt behind the enclosed cab. Not many miles had been covered when the young man was hammering on the back of the cab after realising what was under his feet in the semi-darkness. He was last seen running away from the Land Rover and away from Scotland!

Ted Butt remembers returning to the digs in Worcester (Kempsey) so late one night after a drinking binge that the milkman said good morning to him! Other drivers were rising from their beds as Butty was retiring to his. However, whatever job he would have been on at the time it would have got done. One thing for sure, working for Harris & Miners was never dull. The work could be hard with a lot of "hand ball" loads and great distances to cover, but we played hard as well. A pub was never far away from the chosen digs.

Reg Hill recounted an incident when he was driving before going in the workshop when Alf retired. He had a one-ton pallet for delivery to a factory in the North East, which proved difficult to get rid of. It was urgently required to keep the factory going, so every effort was made to be there quickly to help the customer. On his arrival he was greeted with complete indifference by the forklift driver who appeared to have better things to do than unload one pallet from Reg's trailer and let him get on his way. How many drivers out there have encountered that? I know I have. Two days on Swansea docks once to get rid of 20 tons of clay, Bert Long, Chris Grindling, and Roy Butt were also there. Anyway, after an hour or so Reg rings Brian as he had to get on up the road for a timed delivery. Brian told him to leave and take the pallet with him. As he was pulling out some manager or other came running after him for their 'urgent' pallet. Too late, Reg was having none of it. For the rest of the week that pallet was continually in his way and forever being moved to accommodate the load home. That pallet ended up back in Devon and Brian made them come from the North East and fetch it themselves.

The burnt out remains of a Ford V8 at Ilsington in 1948. Jerry was not amused. (photo: Bill Baty)

Mick Whiteway with Jerry's tipper in 1949. A V8 Ford badged 'Fordson Thames'. These petrol engined Fords were good for 70 m.p.h. empty down hill! (photo: Bill Baty)

Bill Baty in front of the 1946 AEC which Jerry bought from the B.R.S. in 1954. This was one of three AECs bought after denationalisation by Sam and Jerry and this one with the 9.6 litre engine, (the other two had 7.7's and were pre-war), was used to persuade Bill away from B.R.S. and return to Harris & Miners. In its B.R.S. days it was pulling a trailer and as a drawbar outfit the model of AEC was Matador as can be seen on the radiator. The Monarch a non-drawbar 4-wheeler. The Mammouth a 6-wheeler and the 8-wheeler was a Mammouth Major. The tractor units were always Mandators. The Mercury name came in with the Park Royal cabs in the 1950s. Jerry did not buy the trailer as he thought it might complicate things; as a result it would have been a powerful lorry as a 4-wheeler. (photo: Bill Baty)

On the journey to Scotland with the Commer artic in 1954 Mick dropped the trailer in a layby near Beattock and he and wife Ann went camping! (photo: Mick Whiteway)

Harris & Miners driver Jock Addison's wedding in 1962. Brian Harris is standing behind the bride. Others in the picture are all employed by the Company and include; Bill Baty, Mick Whiteway, Ted Butt, Alf Harvey, Gerald Lamb, Gordon Bamsey and Douglas Horrell. (photo: Mick Whiteway)

Ann and Mick at Pill with a Commer tipper. YUO (digits unknown) of 1958 is a QX 7 tonner. (photo: Mick Whiteway)

Eric Whiteway in September 1955 with one of the many Commers to appear on the fleet over the years. Note the window sticker for Widecombe Fair held in September every year. (photo: Bill Baty)

M.C.R. 2.

Summons to Defendant.
(M.C. Act, 1952, s. 1; M.C. Rules, 1952, r. 75.)

In the County of Devon. Petty Sessional Division ~~forxBoxoughx~~of   OTTERY

To   WILLIAM THOMAS FRANK BATY   of

No. 4 Ley Close, Liverton, Newton Abbot.

Information has this day been ~~xxxxxxxxxxxx~~   ~~xxxxxxx~~

         ~~xxxx~~] laid before me, the undersigned Justice of

the Peace, by WILLIAM HARVEY   OF   OTTERY ST.MARY (POLICE SERGEANT)

that you on the   5th   day of   March   19 57,

at   Rockbeare   in the County ~~orxBoroughx~~

[aforesaid] ~~xxxxxxx~~   ] did
unlawfully drive a Heavy Goods Vehicle, on a certain road
called the Exeter-Honiton Main Road, at a speed greater than
20 miles per hour, being the speed specified in the First
Schedule to the Road Traffic Act 1934, as the maximum speed in
relation to a vehicle of that class or description; Contrary
to Section 10 of the Road Traffic Act 1930, as amended by
Section 2 of the Road Traffic Act 1934.

You are therefore hereby summoned to appear on   Tues day the   2nd

day of   April   , 19 57, at the hour of   10.30.

in the   fore noon, before the Magistrates' Court sitting at   The Priory,

Ottery St.Mary   to answer to the said information.

Dated   day   of   March   19 57 ,

Justice of the Peace for the County ~~orxBoroughx~~ [aforesaid] [first above mentioned].

Bill Baty received this summons in 1957 for doing 22 m.p.h. on the A30 trunk road between Exeter and Honiton. How reckless and danerous of him; it's a wonder he was not immediately transported to a penal colony in Australia! This ridiculous 20 m.p.h. speed limit for lorries over 3 tons unladen lingered on to the end of the 1950s.

Dick Barrs roping a load on HTA 742D on one of the rare occasions he was not driving 'Old Faithful'. (photo: Brian Harris)

'Soapy' drove this 6-wheeler for a time which was bought in a hurry to replace a smashed up lorry. (photo: Brian Harris)

The Summer of 1981 sees three of the Brian Harris fleet, still with Harris & Miners on the cab sides, parked in Leith Docks. RSU 'Peter Gurney' was bought second-hand from Reeve and Gossart of Abington in Scotland. Long time friends of Brian's and a great help should there be a mechanical problem when in Scotland. The other two were new to Harris & Miners. (photo: John Henderson)

This Bedford (pictured Christmas 1987) was bought second hand from W.F. Miners of Ashburton for Derek "Birdseye" Webster to drive. "Birdseye" had a heart problem which cost him his Class 1 H.G.V. Licence so he had to come off the artics. He could still drive a 7.5 tonner, however, and big hearted Brian created this job for him to keep him employed. 'Rugglestone Roamer' was eventually replaced by a Roadrunner and "Birdseye" remained with Brian after retirement age and until closure. Another of Brian's drivers was afforded a similar favour and "Soapy" Derek Hudson was also able to continue in employment after health problems took away his Class 1 as well. (photo: John Liddicoat)

Brian bought this ERF 'B' series from friends Reeve and Grossart in Abington on the A74 south of Glasgow. Seen here with a 33 foot trailer at Longcliffe loading clay in October 1983. (photo: Nigel Bunt)

'Dartmoor Raider' in September 1989. A 'C40' 300 Gardner Turbo unit with curtainsider trailer which started to appear on the fleet in the 1980s. Brian's was, however, a largely traditional fleet of flat trailers and they always outnumbered the curtainsiders. (photo: Nigel Bunt)

Billy Baty stands smartly dressed beside the new Leyland Roadtrain in 1983. He was the driver of this lorry while it remained on the fleet; a comparitively short period of 5 years as Brian was offered a good deal to trade it in for another. Extras included spot lights, chrome wheel trims and illuminated headboard, as was the norm for all new lorries. The turnout of the vehicles, from this Devon haulier of modest size, was by now second to none in the country. (photo: Alan Bunting)

Brian Harris stands beside the first Leyland Roadtrain to appear on the fleet in 1983. 'Peter Gurney' was Cummins engined which was an option from the Leyland engine. Paper is being loaded from the store in the yard. (photo: Alan Bunting)

A C40 ERF with Gardner 300 Turbo of 1983. (photo: Nigel Bunt)

'Uncle Tom Cobley' (B149 ATT) at the Hollies on the A5, Cannock, in April 1989. The author remembers staying at the Hollies in his driving days in the 1970s. There was a large room upstairs sleeping twenty or more drivers and at the end of which there was a pipe organ! (photo: Nigel Bunt)

C149 JOD 'Moorland Eagle' loaded with salt from Scunthorpe in 1986 when new. Jimmy Webster was the regular driver of this E12 fitted with a Gardner 270 Turbo 6 cylinder engine and twin-splitter box. (photo: John Liddicoat)

'Moorland Eagle' tipping its load of salt at a tannery in Taunton. (photo: John Liddicoat)

'Dartmoor Jewel' displays the name Jerry on the step. Jerry Snell drove for Brian from the 1980s until closure and usually did a weekly run to the Scottish Highlands. Pictured here in 1989 at Michaelwood. (photo: Nigel Bunt)

Mick Whiteway retired in October 1992 a few days after his 65th birthday, to complete the weeks work. Here he is on retirement day on the Saturday morning at the end of the week finishing a job on a 320 Cummins engine. (photo: Mick Whiteway)

Chapter Eight

THE 1990s – THE DECADE LEADING TO CLOSURE IN 2001

After many good years of trading with plenty of work and a fleet now consisting of thirty-one vehicles there were several hard knocks over the next ten years that little by little sapped Brian's energy, and signalled the beginning of the end for Brian Harris Transport Limited.

For as long as I can remember Brian had been threatening to "shut the gates" and pack up, but we all took it with a pinch of salt; especially as there were no gates to shut! Moaning was his speciality, but by the end of the week it was off to the Welcome Stranger on Friday evenings with many of his drivers, including me, for a skinful of beer and all would be fine again. That was the way of things for decades, in fact many a driver has been known to pull up outside the pub and receive his wages from within. Bert and Doreen ran the place for years and it became affectionately known as Brian's office.

Brian's day book was hand written every day concerning the work done that day, and at the end of each week a summary would be written in the corner of the page which would be categorised either poor week, or very poor week, or very, very poor week, or very, very, very, poor week. I never knew, or saw written down a 'good week' in twenty-five years. However, good times there must have been to enable Brian to have bought new lorries three at a time in the '80s, and then leave them in grey primer parked up at the side of the bottom shed for months before putting them on the fleet. The new ones were usually sprayed by Bovey Commercial Bodies in Pottery Road, a few hundred yards from the depot, and the re-sprays normally carried out by John Fogwill, who rented one of Brian's sheds where he ran, (and still does), his own motor engineering business. John also did all the annual painting carried out before each annual test.

There was always considerable banter between Brian and his staff, and they were continually shouting at each other, but it was normally good humoured, and even if a blazing row had taken place with one of his men it was usually forgotten soon afterwards. On one occasion Brian was in a particularly bad mood and threatened to close the place yet again, when his senior fitter, Reg Hill, called his bluff. Reg came off the road in 1983 to go in the workshops and was there until the end. He replaced Mick Whiteway who had come off the road many years before to go into the workshop and he was there in the beginning. Anyway, Brian had just ordered some spare parts from Frank Tucker in Exeter, (the ERF agents until a few years ago), after which Reg immediately picked up the phone in front of Brian and rang Tuckers to cancel the spares because "Brian's closing down". It all went quiet for a time after that and we didn't hear quite so much about closure for a while.

However, the storm clouds were gathering through the 1990s and Brian's face was beginning to show the strain of running the company virtually single-handed. On 5th July 1991 Candy Tiles went into receivership with the loss of 220 staff. This was a business at Heathfield, Newton Abbot, which had been a customer of Harris & Miners, and Brian Harris, since 1947. That cost Brian £90,000 and the debt was never paid. There had been several loads a week out of the factory that meant a lot more work had to be found elsewhere. All credit to Brian, not a single driver was laid off and the fleet remained the same strength. It was, however, five years before another new lorry was bought. There were also two eight-wheeler tippers to find work for as Brian also had the contract for taking raw materials, such as flint and clay, into Candy Tiles. Then a couple of years later Candy was started up again under new management and a revamped name, so Brian was back doing their haulage once again. That did not last long and it all went pear-shaped again taking Brian for another huge sum of money. £40,000 this time!

At about this time Brian lost a contract from a paper mill in Ivybridge, Devon, through no fault of his own. After thirty years of carrying their paper to Scotland he was taken to lunch one day and told his services were no longer required due to a re-organisation of transport within the company. In other words, someone else got all their work, including Scotland. He also lost the transport from a firm in Ilminster, Somerset, making industrial heaters as a result of a similar shake-up. This time he did not get offered lunch, just a 'phone call. This was another company Brian had been hauling for thirty years. These three customers accounted for a fair chunk of Brian's direct work – as opposed to sub-contracting through another haulier, – and in spite of other setbacks still to come, Brian has told me he would still be in business if he still had their work.

For years the work had come to Brian just by picking up the 'phone. He virtually had the traffic from Devon and Cornwall to Scotland and the North East to himself. Very few of his competitors in the Southwest wanted to go that far north, as they had no contacts for back loads. Brian, and his father before him, had been going to Scotland since 1948 and had built up a considerable customer base north of the border. Loads out of Scotland would be kept for Brian. He had it to himself. Not only were loads kept for Brian, they were kept for a specific driver. "Aye, that'll be Tony Taylor's load for Friday" came the answer from one traffic manager to me at a Scottish paper mill that we regularly loaded out of. In those days Brian even had three drivers living in Scotland. Sundays would regularly see six or eight lorries heading north, but that got fewer in recent years as work dried up. Sometimes lorries would leave with only half a load just to get them up to Scotland to keep customers up there happy.

Times in the mid-1990s were considerably harder and Brian had ceased to enjoy work, it showed on his face. Five years old second-hand ERFs now replaced the ten years old ones instead of being replaced with new ones. Friends and colleagues suggested Brian ought to take on someone to help with the traffic and take some responsibility, so Brian would not be completely tied to the yard as he was seven days a week. Back in the 1970s Brian would go to Scotland once a year to see his customers and do some serious drinking with them. This, however, had all stopped as he became trapped in his own business, because only he had the knowledge of what was going on. If anyone wants to work seven days a week then that is fine by me as long as they are happy doing it. Billy Baty was taken off the road in 1995 with the idea of training him to take over some of Brian's horrendous workload. Brian was running a fleet of thirty-one lorries on his own with the result that practically all day and every day was spent on the 'phone just trying to keep them moving. There was seldom any time to stand back and look at the business. And all this was achieved with two telephones, (one would be taken off the hook if Brian left the office even to go to the toilet), a fax, and pen and paper. Anyone calling on him must have wondered what on earth was going on. A 'phone in each hand; drivers and customers all demanding answers at the same time. A breakdown to be dealt with, a late delivery to be investigated, a decision to be made on a lorry with engine trouble in the workshop. "Park the bloody thing out the back" would often be the retort. With the rough treatment Brian gave the phones they never lasted very long! Such was the delightfully old fashioned way of running things that only a handful of lorries even had 'phones in them, although Brian usually had a pretty good idea where most of his drivers were at any time. He was once asked if he "went continental", to which he answered he had a hard enough time finding his drivers in this country without having to find them spread all over Europe!

The lack of modern technology was very quaint and I admire the way Brian ran such a fleet with barely anything written down for so long, but there was a downside. I know that when I was "on the books" in the '70s none of us had 'phones because no one had invented them yet, (heaven). But times had changed and companies had to change with them or be left behind. Gordon Bamsey drove one of the blue ERF artics, M393 NNC 'Bill Brewer', with a crane mounted behind the cab for farm machinery deliveries. On one particular trip he telephoned Brian from his last drop somewhere in Cambridgeshire to be told to head north to Yorkshire for a load, as there was nothing where he was. Within half an hour of leaving and heading up the A1 empty, a back load was offered from East Anglia. But he was out of contact.

Things were going to change announced Brian to John, then the landlord of the Cromwell Arms in Bovey Tracey, a favourite watering hole at the time. Billy would take on more so Brian could take it easier and maybe even get to Scotland for a few days. In the five years Billy was off the road and in the yard, the nearest he ever got to running the office was answering the 'phone if Brian had to go to the doctor, (his health was suffering under the pressure and he is diabetic), or whatever. Billy spent those final years working for Brian in the yard building fences, helping in the workshops, and doing the odd bit of local driving, but was never given that responsibility in the office that I know Billy could have done so well. He had been with Brian for over thirty years and "knew the ropes". So nothing changed. When push came to shove I do not think either Brian or Margaret had it in them to relinquish any responsibility and let someone else make any decisions, even though Billy is a cousin of Brian, and his father Bill was a decision maker on the firm and ran the office for Jerry forty years before. Margaret kept things very close to her chest and even the two staff at Widecombe, who did the book keeping in a room of the house Brian shared with his mother, were not privy to the whole picture. Dartmoor folk are a bit like that, you know.

Another change that never got off the ground was the introduction of computers in 2000. A decision was made to move the bookkeeping side of things to the depot in Bovey Tracey and relieve Margaret of some of the burden (she is 86). A portacabin was positioned in the yard and re-furbished by Billy. It was then moved as the original site was against the wall of the paint shop right next to the extractor fan! £3,000 worth of computers was put in place and a man who could work them turned up. Derek had worked for H.J.T. transport up until their closure in April 2000. He had been employed in their office and was used to all aspects of business being stored on computers. He started on a Monday morning. On Tuesday he went to Widecombe to get the information needed to load into the computer, which Margaret did not feel inclined to disclose. On Wednesday he left. The computers remained dormant. It's that Dartmoor thing again.

So the company was to continue in the way it always had. Widecombe-in-the-Moor remained the registered office and Margaret now appeared in the yard every day to watch over the bookkeepers! At 86 she has to be admired for the way she kept the company such a personal possession. Only she and Brian ever really knew anything about it.

In 1998/9 incomers into new houses built opposite, and down the road from the yard started making a fuss to the local council and the district council (Teignbridge), about living next door to a transport business and the associated noises that go with it. They bought the houses knowing what was next door didn't they? What do they expect if houses are built on top of an industrial site? The whole of Pottery Road had for generations been industrial. Potteries would you believe. Harris & Miners had operated from one of the old pottery sites since 1957 and Brian Harris from the same site since 1978. Apart from pottery workers' cottages there were no houses anywhere near the yard. Nevertheless this neighbourly bad feeling towards Brian resulted in jobsworths from the District Council – the local Parish Council was on Brian's side – descending on his yard with all the fervour only councils know how to muster. Men in suits appeared with sound meters listening for every little noise that might upset the incomers. Admittedly Brian had not helped his own cause over the years as the yard had seen little investment and the somewhat potholed surface of the yard was not conducive to silent running in and out. Dust in the summer and mud in the winter were the norm. Brian's theory being that the yard did not earn the money, the lorries did. The compressor was consigned to a sound proof box, and eight-foot high fences were erected between the boundary and the new houses to protect their occupants from the sight and sound of the nasty, smelly lorries. Brian is not an unreasonable man and bent over backwards to appease his neighbours and keep them happy as much as he could, but a transport yard is what it is, a place of work.

The Teignbridge Council were not interested that he had been on the site before the houses were built, only that they had had complaints. Injunctions were slapped on the yard restricting the movements of lorries to within certain times. Nothing could enter or leave before 7.00 a.m. or after 7.00 p.m. Nothing after midday on Saturday, and Sunday working confined to just two hours from 9.00 a.m. to 11.00 a.m. Transport does not work like that and freight needs to be moved at the customer's demand and in their time day or night.

The sad fact was that this unwarranted intrusion into the operations of Brian Harris Transport was another factor leading to its closure. The Council wanted Brian to move to new premises on the Heathfield Industrial Estate, just outside Bovey Tracey. However, Brian is 58 years old and has no family to continue the business, (he has never married). He lives with his mother (now well into her eighties) in Widecombe-in-the-Moor and everything is paid for. Why then, with this set of circumstances should he involve himself with the up-heaval of moving and starting all over again? It is also no secret that Margaret wanted him to call it a day as his health was buckling under the strain. A friend of mine, David Jewitt, had a business dealing in second-hand tractors and used the services of Brian Harris to move them about the country until his own health let him down with a heart attack. He said to Brian that if he (Brian) did not pack it in it was going to kill him. To which Brian answered, "I know".

The foot and mouth epidemic which started in February 2001 was probably the final straw as four lorries were almost full-time engaged in the transport of farm machinery for Western Machinery, of Ivybridge, Devon. Lorries specially equipped with cranes – the blue fleet – for the task of self-unloading at agricultural machinery dealers and county shows. The orders dried up and the movements stopped. More lorries to find work for. For the first time in the company's history a trading loss appeared on the balance sheet. The suggestion from friends and colleagues to either employ someone to turn the business around, or slim it down to a fleet of a more manageable size was dismissed by Brian and Margaret. It was not an option to start making some drivers redundant in order to reduce the fleet. Brian had had an offer a few years ago to buy him out, but when he asked about the drivers' security and was told they were not needed, he declined the offer. It was all or nothing. As he said, "If I can't run it my way then its time to pack it in". Modern practises, events, and circumstances meant that he could no longer run it "his way". Brian was also too much of a gentleman to get out there in the market place and fight for business.

So it was then, that on Friday 30th March 2001 at 5.00 p.m. he announced that he was closing down with just one weeks notice. While a lot of us knew things were not as rosy as they had been it still came as a considerable shock. At least one driver, Peter Rees, the longest serving with thirty-five years to his credit, learnt of his fate in Tesco's the following day! Others who had got there first told others as they returned to the yard. I had been sign writing a trailer the day before for Brian, so received the news from a third party with utter disbelief. I think Brian was so embarrassed by events that he could not bring himself to give more notice, and even customers heard of the closure from drivers and outsiders. George Coker, who had been an owner-driver operating out of Brian's yard a few years before, told me over the 'phone two days later. The company ceased trading the following Friday, 6th April, and the last lorry ran into the yard on Sunday morning 8th April, returning from Scotland.

I trust it was after 9.00 a.m. and before 11.00 a.m.

Ted Saunders had this 4-wheeler new in 1987. It had a 6 litre 180 Cummins engine with 8-speed gearbox. (photo: John Liddicoat)

'Devon Chieftain' on the road in April 1989. B71 WDV originally had a 300 Turbo Gardner engine but this seized and it was replaced with a Cummins unit from an Atki which necessitated a consideravble amount of plumbing to make it fit. (photo: Nigel Bunt)

The 'Old Grey Mare' northbound M6, Michaelwood services 1987. (photo: Nigel Bunt)

The second of the Leyland Roadtrains to appear on the fleet loading clay at English China Clays, Wareham, for Dalry in Ayrshire with Billy Baty in charge. (photo: Brian Harris Collection)

Bryn Jones took this load of heaters from Powrmatic to Paisley. Derek Ellis (Del Boy) was the regular driver at that time. He was driver of the latest 'T' registered lorry when Brian closed down. The DUMB sign spelt something unprintable! (photo: Brian Harris Collection)

D932 POD, 'Dartmoor Poacher', was new to Reg Hill in 1986. Seen here with a full load of paper. (photo: John Liddicoat)

Tony Taylor had 'Tom Pearce' when new in 1986. He was known as the Falkirk Flyer as that was his regular weekly run. Photographed in the yard by Dave Lee.

'Old Grey Mare' looking a picture at the Royal Showground with a load of Western Machinery from Ivybridge. The trailer was re-painted at the same time when the pair were 8 years old. (photo: Iean MacKenzie)

The original driver of this lorry, Ian 'Jock' Brand died of a heart attack while delivering to a dealer in government surplus equipment in the Teign valley. A stressful occasion arose in a narrow lane and he got out of the cab to sort it out and dropped dead, three weeks before Christmas 1989. Although the lorry was practically new at the time no-one on the firm would drive it. Gary Ball joined Brian Harris on January 1st 1990 and not knowing the history took it on and remained with Brain until closure and bought this unit to preserve at the auction. It remains in Bovey Tracey. (photo: Dave Brewer)

December 1988 somewhere in Devon judging by the sign to the left of the lorry which asks drivers to keep the county tidy. 'Uncle' was driven by Ted Saunders who lived in Scotland (and still does in retirement). 'Uncle' was an endearment to Jerry Harris. (photo: Nigel Bunt)

A stage managed photograph for the 1999 Brian Harris calendar that was sent to all his customers at Christmas. A lovely Dartmoor scene with Haytor Rock in the background. (photo: Duncan Shear)

'Widecombe Pixie' was driven by Ted Butt 'Butty' as can be seen from the name on the step. Seen here in 1989 next to a W.F. Miners Scania. This company from Ashburton in Devon had no business connection with Harris & Miners, as is often assumed. (photo: Nigel Bunt)

A publicity shot for Western Machinery at the Royal Showgrond at Stoneleigh in Warwickshire. Iean MacKenzie with E792 BFJ and Gordon Bamsey with G403 OVM, 'Old Grey Mare' and 'Jan Stewer'. (photo: Iean MacKenzie)

Gordon Bamsey had 'Jan Stewer' when new to the company. Seen here with a load of Western Machinery from Ivybridge. Gordon joined Harris & Miners in 1964 aged 21. (photo: Brian Harris Collection)

Phil Bolt parked up with this Cummins engined Seddon Atkinson. (photo: Brian Harris Collection)

G496 WDV photographed at Wye Commercials after the auction. Brian always ran at least one drop sided 8-wheeler that could be used for a tipping load in one direction and mixed load in the other. An E10 Cummins engined ERF with sleeper cab, 'Widecombe Lad' was on the fleet from new until closure. (photo: Nigel Bunt)

'Dartmoor Lady' was driven when new by 'Jock' Phil Wilde who remained with the Company until closure. Seen here sitting in the yard in September 1989. The trailer was fitted with a crane to unload the industrial heaters from Powrmatic concealed beneath the sheets. Brian did all the Scottish work for this Company for 30 years but the loss of this customer (through no fault of Brian) was one of the factors in the decision to close down. (photo: Nigel Bunt)

'Peter Davey' on a winter's night in March 1989. (photo: Nigel Bunt)

Downside, Dundee sees three of the fleet loaded with paper for Bristol. (photo: John Liddicoat)

Warren "Brummy" Piggot with K151 GSO missing its name plate. It was 'Knight of the Moor' and remained with the same driver until closure. (photo: Brian Harris Collection)

D932 POD, 'Dartmoor Poacher', was new to Reg Hill in 1986. Seen here with a full load of paper. It is a delight to see an expertly sheeted and roped load such as this. These traditional lorry driver's skills are fast disappearing. (photo: John Liddicoat)

L419 RDM 'Daniel Whiddon' was new to B.O.C.D.S. and bought by Bryn Jones who operated as an owner-driver out of Brian's yard. He subsequently sold the lorry to Brian and remained as a driver for Brian until the end. It made £4,000 at the auction. (photo: Nigel Bunt)

L965 NAO 'Dartmoor Viking' in the yard on 17.3.01. An EC14-41TT bought second hand by Brian. He never bought any 6x2 units new. (photo: Nigel Bunt)

M448 VER in the yard in March 2001. An EC14-41ST ERF 6x2 tractor. This one was uprated from 340 to 380 with mid-lift on air with tipping gear. Quite a rarity for the fleet as Brian never bought any new units on either air suspension or with tipping gear. The trailer was rented. This lorry remained unnamed. (photo: Nigel Bunt)

Kenny Binks southbound on the M5. 'Dartmoor Laddie' of the blue fleet. An ERF EC14. The 14 litre Cummins is now out of production as it no longer meets the stringent EC regulations for exhaust emissions.
(photo: Brian Harris Collection)

A cheery wave from Andy Pointon coming down Haldon Hill. (photo: Brian Harris Collection)

Iean MacKenzie opposite the Dome with another load of drilling rig equipment in year 2000. Although missing its name plate this ERF bought second hand by Brian was called 'The Old Grey Mare' which was the name of Iean's previous lorry, E792 BFJ. A few months later M672 YSW was to sell for £6,500, being a 6x2 tractor. One of the very few lorries that Brian did not have an illuminated headboard fitted. (photo: Iean MacKenzie)

Gweek, near Helston, 3 Brian Harris artics loaded with a drilling rig for the north of Scotland. From one end of the British Isles to the other. Iean MacKenzie and Warren Piggot stand by their lorries while the driver of C614 JTA, Bart (Mark Bartholomew) took the picture. (photo: Iean MacKenzie)

A load of Powrmatic heaters from Somerset heading up the A74 in Scotland at Cairn Lodge. The exact date is unknown but the advertised price of a litre of petrol at 57.9 pence puts it a few years ago. Phil 'Jock' Wilde proudly shows the Scottish flag on the rear of his trailer. (photo: Brian Harris Collection)

The Lord Mayor's Show on Plymouth Hoe. B71 proudly shows off its new paint. Nigel Trout was by now the driver of this lorry and he kept it until it came off the road in 1999. (photo: Brian Harris Collection)

'Soapy' took this overhanging load of oil rig legs to Scotland. When pulling onto Southwaite services for the night he forgot what was above the cab and rammed the back of a container lorry; the driver of which was thrown out of his bunk by the force. He must have thought it was an earthquake for the next thing 'Soapy' saw was a naked man (save for his underpants) running around the services in a state of panic! (photo: Brian Harris Collection)

Load after load of drilling rigs went from Cornwall to the far north of Scotland during the 1990s and Brian Harris Transport Limited was the haulier for the task. (photo: Brian Harris Collection)

A Euclid machine from Newhouse in Scotland for St. Austell in Cornwall. Brian's drivers certainly had to cope with a wide range of loads. Who is doing this sort of mixed traffic on flat trailers now? (photo: Brian Harris Collection)

Another part of a drilling rig from Falmouth leaves the Bovey Tracey depot heading for the north of Scotland in 1987 with "Grizzly" at the wheel. (photo: John Liddicoat)

Kevin Discombe drove this 6x2 two tone blue ERF with a crane mounted behind the cab. Unusually a lorry with no name! Seen here with a grain dryer from Law Dennis at Yate for Scotland. (photo: Brian Harris Collection)

The trombone trailer extended to 60 feet on Brixham Quay. Howard Marine of Plymouth had supplied these pontoon legs for harbour improvements at Brixham and they are now on their way to Whitehaven in the north east of Scotland. (photo: Brian Harris Collection)

Graham "Swivel" Perkins taking part in the fuel protest in Newton Abbot passing through Newfoundland Way in September 2000. Did the Government listen? (photo: Brian Harris Collection)

Brian Harris taking delivery of P680 YTT from Duncan Shears in the yard at Bovey Tracey in the Summer of 1996. (photo: Brian Harris Collection)

'Dartmoor Jewel' at the 1987 Royal Cornwall show. An E14 (14 litre Cummins) ERF. (photo: Nigel Bunt)

John Fogwill has been associated with Brian for many years as a motor engineer running his own business from premises in Brian's yard. He helped in the workshop when required and did most of the servicing of the lorries and trailers for their annual test. His father also helped him and Brian and did a lot of relief driving as well. John built and raced Minis with considerable success and was sponsored by Brian so the cars were in Brian Harris colours. John is no longer racing but continues to run his garage rented from Brian. He still services the author's family's cars. (photo: Brian Harris Collection)

T470 AFJ 'Dartmoor Avenger' was the last new lorry to be bought by Brian and the one the Corgi model was based on. Seen here at the Truck Fest at Shepton Mallet in 1999. (photo: Brian Harris Collection)

A new 'Peter Gurney' awaits registration. October 1988 in the yard at Bovey Tracey. (photo: Nigel Bunt)

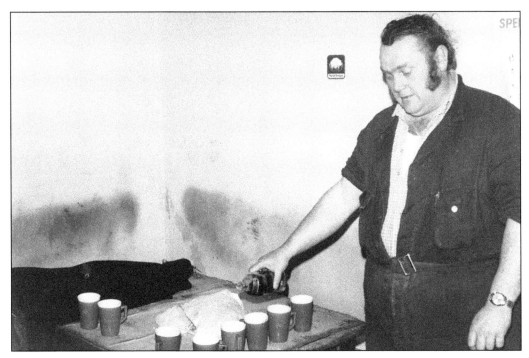

All the drivers had their own blue mug from Liverton Pottery with names on them. Only two in this picture can be seen, they are Alf and Lenny. This tradition carried on for many years whilst Alf's wife worked at the pottery. Tea was the usual tipple but Christmas was when Brian would give every man a mug of whisky before the beer-up at the Welcome Stranger. (photo: Bill Baty)

A typical grey day on Dartmoor. The road from Widecombe to Bovey Tracey shows off this ERF E14 with a load of Western Machinery for the 2001 Calendar. (photo: Duncan Shear)

Chapter Nine

WEDNESDAY 18th APRIL 2001. THE AUCTION

Friday 30th March 2001; Brian announces closure.
Friday 6th April 2001; Brian Harris Transport Limited ceases trading.
Sunday 8th April 2001; last lorry returns home from Scotland driven by 'Jock' Phil Wilde.
Wednesday 18th April 2001; the auction.

Just nineteen days separated events from the 5.00 p.m. brief statement from Brian that he was closing down, to everything being sold off. And just ten days separated the arrival of the last lorry back in the yard to the end of the auction and all the lorries leaving the yard for the last time. All credit must go to Wye Valley Commercials Limited of Ross-on-Wye for the excellent way in which they presented the auction in such a short time. Also to the auctioneer, Chris Wright of C.V.A. Doncaster, who knew exactly how to extract every penny out of the bidders.

Wye Commercials had little over a week to set up the sale and arrange the lots for auction. A task they had not done before on such a scale, but one that they threw themselves into to help Brian. He had been a good customer over the years, buying many second-hand tractors and trailers from them, and they repaid that loyalty in a very special way. The presentation on the day was first class.

Three hundred catalogues were sent out to prospective buyers and on the day there were 197 registered. On the first day of the announcement of the sale four 'phone lines were permanently kept busy for four hours non-stop. Every lot was for sale with no reserves except the ERF, 373 FOD, which had a reserve of £8,000. This was the first ERF on the fleet in 1960 and the only one Brian had no intentions of selling. It was, however, a good draw on the day and reached a bid of £5,250, (from Stan Robinson of Stoke-on-Trent), and remained unsold. The other lorry in the vintage section was a Thames Trader, registration 32 MDV, lot number 168. It made £250 and was bought by a driver from Poole in Dorset for restoration. This lorry was bought by Jerry Harris for Brian to drive, on the first of January 1963 with a payload of 9.5 tons. I am reliably informed by Reg Hill that a load of 13 tons was not uncommon! When Brian took over the running of the business from his father it was parked up, when only a few years old, and never turned a wheel again until it was dragged away after the auction.

Lot numbers 1 to 99 were various artefacts appertaining to the running of a haulage business, such as workshop equipment, sheets, ropes, chains, and straps etc. Also included in this section were the yard shunter and a pair of units in bits. Lot numbers 93 and 94 were two Seddon Atkinson units long past their usefulness (were they ever useful?) which fetched £1,500 the pair and the ERF shunter, HAD 949V, with a 265 Rolls Eagle diesel made £500. This tractor unit had been swapped some years before for a Gardner engined shunter with an export value to Africa. HAD 949V turned up in the yard as a replacement for yard shunting duties and Brian noticed that it still had a few months test on it, so it was immediately put to work. Nigel Trout was given the task of driving it to Scotland and back for as long as it would keep going! It finally died in North Devon with a broken prop shaft and returned to the yard to finish its days as the workshop hack. I assume with another prop shaft.

The first of the trailers went under the hammer as lot 110. A mixture of mostly flat 40 footers of Tasker or Crane Fruehauf origin, and eight curtainsiders of 40 and 45 foot length, of assorted manufacture. There were also step-frame low loaders and a "trombone" trailer which extended to 60 feet for abnormal loads, of which Brian did many between the South West and the North East of Scotland for the offshore oil industry. Although many of the trailers were built in the mid-1980s they were in exceptional condition and that was reflected in the excellent prices they made. Brian's policy of re-painting them every year, and very largely keeping unit, trailer, and driver together as much as possible saw to that.

Lot number 135 began the opening bid on the lorries with the rigids preceding the artic units, and the two vintage ones completing the sale at 3.00 p.m. The early spring sunshine showed them all off to full advantage. Every one of them had had their chassis re-painted prior to annual testing, so the older 12 to 14 years old motors had visited the paint shop 12 to 14 times and I had put back the coach lines and lettering as necessary 12 to 14 times on each one! Find me another fleet with such attention to detail and pride in appearance. A bit of a joke with the Ministry Testing Station on the Marsh Barton Industrial Estate in Exeter was that Brian's fitters must have used a spanner size bigger to everyone else to compensate for the thickness of paint! It paid off in the end though, as was evident in the prices realised at auction.

There were a number of 'F' registered units to be sold at the auction that had all just finished a week's work earning their keep on distance work. Many were still tramping the roads to Scotland and back right up to the last day of operations. 1,800 miles a week of hard graft on vehicles well over 10 years old. A couple went to a dealer in Yorkshire; one went to Cornwall and is now used to pull a low loader with the owner's steamroller. It is staying in Brian's colours, with his permission, and is regularly seen during the summer months at steam engine rallies. One has been retained by one of Brian's ex-drivers. Gary Ball drove this one, F513 MOD, when he first joined Brian Harris some eight years previously. It originally sold at the auction for £1,000 to the Yorkshire dealer, which was all Gary could afford but we missed it. However, with a little help from Chris Simons, a philanthropic local, a deal was struck and the ERF tractor unit remains in Bovey Tracey in retirement.

A combination of factors kept prices of many of the lorries rather low. There was no shortage of buyers as they had come from all parts of the country including Scotland and Northern Ireland. Jock McBean came from Scotland and I think bought three units. Then came the problem of getting home, so he bought a curtain sided trailer to put his car in! An 'N' registered ERF unit, N155 TDV made £5,500 and left that afternoon to catch a ferry for Northern Ireland. However, there were some bargains to be had and I imagine one of those factors would have been the ridiculous amount of tax this government extracts from hauliers in the form of fuel duty; it has certainly depressed the industry. It also appeared that 'K', 'L', and 'M' registered four-wheel ERF tractor units on steel springs with twin-splitter gearboxes are not everyone's choice. K151 GSO with Cummins 14 litre '410' and Jake brake made a derisory £1,750. It was a well looked after motor driven by Warren 'Brummy' up to closure. I had driven it on several occasions when coupled to Brian's tandem axle beaver tailed step-frame to carry the Leyland Octopus tanker, (ex-Taunton Cider of 1949 vintage), to shows up and down the country. It was a joy to drive and I was tempted to buy it myself, but fortunately managed to keep my hands firmly in my pockets! Lots 141, 142, and 143 made just over £3,000 between them. 'E' and 'F' registered ERF 4x2 units, two of which had already come off the road, have gone to Trevor Whitfield of Collumpton in Devon to begin new lives on recovery and shunting duties. He already has an 'A' Series ERF recovery vehicle.

The lorry on which the Corgi model was based found a new home with W.J. Clayton of Rogerstone, Risca, in South Wales. Lot 164, T470 AFJ, an ERF EC11 made £20,000. Less than two years old and with an extended warranty until July 2004 for substantially under half-price than when new. It was the most recent vehicle on the fleet. Lot 166 at £21,750 was the highest price paid for any of the lorries and was bought by Kay Transport of Plympton, Devon. M393 NNC is an ERF EC14 twin-steer 6x2 unit on air fitted with a

1997 Palfinger crane behind the cab. Gordon Bamsey had been the driver of this one on farm machinery deliveries for Western Farm Machinery of Ivybridge, one of Brian's longstanding customers. Gordon went to school with Brian and had over thirty years service, in two instalments, with the company.

The two final lots of the day were the vintage lorries. The Thames Trader will hopefully be restored by its new owner and the ERF, which Brian has kept for himself, is at present the subject of a £20,000 plus rebuild in Shropshire. The sale realised a creditable £400,000. During the entire day, and until after the hammer had come down for the last time, Brian remained in his office and away from proceedings. There was a steady flow of old friends and colleagues popping in to see him throughout the day and a tear or two was shed by the man himself over the passing of a lifetime's work. After the business had been done he emerged to chat with everyone and even permitted me to take his photograph by one of his now ex-lorries. I had been covering the auction for "Truck and Driver" magazine and had been busy with my camera all day. After the company had ceased trading Brian kept on two of his most loyal employees until after the auction to help with the considerable amount of work involved in getting everything ready and moved around, as well as clearing up at the end of it all. Reg Hill and Gordon Bamsey had over sixty years service between them with Harris & Miners, and Brian Harris Transport. Nothing was too much trouble for them and they worked hard in the twelve days prior to the auction, and were also a considerable help to Wye Commercials on the day. By about 6.00 p.m. most of the lorries had left for their new homes and from a full and bustling yard it now looked very empty and rather sad. As there were no reserves (except 373 FOD) there was nothing left unsold.

So, there we were. Brian and a few of his colleagues, including Phil Hoskin of Parsons Transport from Exeter, who bought several lots including a couple of units, and two or three trailers. Phil has been a good friend to Brian over the years and was a great help through this difficult period. Brian Burson and his son, and son-in-law were there, so were Reg, Gordon, John Liddicoat, and I.

We all went to the pub!

Chapter Ten

POST BRIAN HARRIS TRANSPORT LIMITED

After the events of 18th April 2001 Reg Hill and Gordon Bamsey had a week spent clearing up the yard before they too were paid off and there was nobody left, except Brian, in an empty space once occupied by a thriving transport business since 1957. There was obviously several months' work left winding up the company and finalising the accounts. The portacabin was still occupied by John Edworthy until August sorting out all that had to be done. The drivers and fitters all received what redundancy was owed them within a few weeks and the company was wound up with all accounts settled. There was never any question of "going bust". The fact was Brian and his mother had had enough of the daily grind. When the company ceased trading on 6th April there was £500,000 owed to it and there was no overdraft. Several lorries were on finance but funds were sufficient to pay it all off.

Brian bought himself a new pick-up which drew the comment from Reg, "I see you're spending your redundancy!"

As far as I know all the drivers and fitters have found new employment. Anyone who had worked for Brian is highly regarded in the industry, as he commanded a lot of respect. Brian keeps in touch with many of them by 'phone on a regular basis and there was a reunion in December last year. Brian was there at the Keyberry Inn, Newton Abbot, mixing with his old staff. Although none of them liked losing their job, none of them bears a grudge. It was very much a unique operation with a boss who knew his men intimately. At the Christmas Eve lunchtime party he would be at the centre of it, never aloof like so many employers throwing a party because it was expected of them. Although there were hard times they were outnumbered by the good times. What everybody misses is the togetherness, the gossip, the being part of the family. This extended to outsiders as well. John Fogwill who did much of the painting, Ian Crook the electrician. He was always about at least once during the week and every Saturday morning. He was very often trying to do some wiring on a lorry when I was trying to signwrite it, so we had a love/hate relationship! He is a fellow biker so he is not all bad. John Fogwill senior still helped here and there. Ted Butt, Bill Baty, Mick and Ann Whiteway, the list goes on. It was like a community centre with lorries!

So, what of the yard? Brian is still there most days of the week keeping abreast with the outside world and keeping an interest in transport. Although no longer running any lorries he is doing a bit of outside storage and organising transport on a clearing house basis. He is happy and now has a smile back on his face. He has time to talk and has recently been a great help to me in getting this book finished. His memory is amazing and has been able to reel off registration numbers of lorries of forty years ago! I am sure his health has improved since the burden of running over thirty lorries has gone. In the early days of Harris & Miners the long distances involved in going to Scotland were the making of the company, but with ever increasing costs it became harder to sustain. The last month of trading ran up a fuel bill of £84,000. Every month that fuel was paid for in advance.

Apart from Brian's outside storage he has let out the rest of the yard he is not using, and all the buildings on a 5 years lease to several different concerns. A housing estate one day maybe, but not for a few years while Brian still keeps active by being there. John Fogwill still has his garage where he has been for many years, where the original workshop was situated. A vehicle recovery business is using part of the yard for storing accident-damaged cars. A dealer in used trucks and vans is in another part, and buildings have been rented by Bovey Truck and Van Bodies, formerly Bovey Commercials who made many lorry bodies for Brian over the years and did most of his accident repairs.

The injunction slapped on Brian Harris Transport Limited, which curtailed his movements to within certain hours as a result of complaints from local residents only applied to that company. Brian could have started another haulage business under another name from that site with no restrictions using existing planning consent. He knew it and the local council knew it, which is why a change of use was so readily granted from a transport business to industrial premises. Some residents had complained bitterly about living near a transport yard and succeeded in various restrictions being imposed. Albeit the yard was there first. The noise and movement in and out of that transport yard was nothing to the activities of a commercial body building company, a second-hand commercial vehicle dealer, and a vehicle recovery business.

Oh, I nearly forgot, a demolition contractor is also renting part of the yard. I do hope the residents are pleased with themselves.

The auctioneer taking bids for the trailers. (photo: Author)

Ted Butt and 'Old Faithful' pose for the camera on auction day. Ted started with the company when this ERF was new in 1960. (photo: Author)

December 2001 and the restoration of 373 FOD is under way at C & G. Coachworks, Much Wenlock in Shropshire. (photo: John & Neil Boughey)

Chapter Eleven

MOVING ON

Since Brian closed his business in 2001 a lot has changed in the road haulage industry, and not always for the better. Other traditional hauliers that were operating at the time of Brian Harris closing down have now also given up the struggle and closed. Names such as Gibbs of Frazerborough, Hinchliffe of Bury, and George Holladay of Penrith to name but three associated with Brian Harris Transport. We have also lost Torbay Freight from my local area (and another customer of mine). The big players with their depots all over the country and central 'hubs' in the Midlands appear to have taken over at the expense of the traditional and family run concerns; but are these big operators making any money? It is so competitive out there that margins are very small and since the manufacturing base of this country has largely gone the need for general haulage has diminished. Just look at what goes up and down the motorways in comparison to twenty years ago. It now seems that a supermarket owns every other lorry going by! Those that are not have given themselves fancy titles, which include words such as "logistics". Where have all the flat trailers with sheeted loads gone? Come to think of it, where has the traditionally sign-written lorry gone? All mostly consigned to history. Brian Harris is best out of it as he nearly always says whenever I see him. Today's way of doing things is so different to the way Brian operated when he and his contemporaries called themselves 'transport contractors' or 'hauliers'. And they ran lorries, not trucks!

One lorry that Brian ran was bought new by Harris & Miners in 1960 and it is the one that did not make its reserve at the auction. In fact, Brian had no intentions of letting it go as plans were already in place to restore it. 373 FOD "*Happy Wanderer*", or "*Old Faithful*" as the KV ERF 4-wheeler became better known by was collected shortly afterwards. John and Neil Boughy of C & G Coachworks, Much Wenlock, took on a four-year restoration between 2001 and 2005. Brian kept telling me it would be ready for the next rally season and that I would be taking it. Entry forms were sent off for the 2003 and 2004 Bournemouth to Colerne (Bath) Runs, but we finally made it for the 2005 event. Various delays in the restoration process were overcome and "*Happy Wanderer*" came back to Devon in August 2005 to make its debut at the Widecombe-in-the-Moor Primary School Fete on the 13th of that month, just 24 hours after returning from an excellent job by the Boughy father and son team. I was privileged to drive it on the Bournemouth to Colerne (Bath) Run on the first Sunday of September three weeks later where it won best in show and best in its class. Twenty-five years had slipped by since I last drove that lorry and it felt like only yesterday. Gary Ball kept me company as he took along his ERF unit bought at the auction and now repainted, kindly paid for by Brian.

Gary not only looks after his own lorry but has also taken on the responsibility of looking after the KV for Brian and takes it to various shows. I get to play with it occasionally and was told at one event that I had it made!

"How's that?"
"Well," said the very astute observer, "You get the fun of driving Brian's lorry while he puts the diesel into it for you, and Gary cleans it."

Seems like a good arrangement to me, especially so as at the time I was in the beer tent and Gary was outside polishing.

On a sadder note we lost Mick Whiteway towards the end of 2006. He had been the longest serving member of staff, having joined Harris & Miners in 1946. He had been a great help to me in writing the first edition.

There have also been a loss of one or two other ex-Harris & Miners drivers since the closure of the company and since the book was first published: Bert Long, Charlie Martin, Jerry Snell, Bill Mortimore, and Maurice Pickford have all passed away. I was privileged to have known them all and worked with them. Characters of the haulage business that will never be replaced as the era they knew has gone forever. To these men I dedicate this second edition.

They, and I, lived through an era of roping and sheeting, crash gearboxes, pre-Motorways, and booking digs for the night. We never moaned if the lorry had no radio or heater, or sleeper cab. No mobile phones or tachographs forever checking up on us; we got on with the job. At the end of the week we all had a beer or two together and met up on the road during the next week's work. Has the industry got better for the driver? I think not.

Those of us that were privileged to have been drivers in the days of Harris & Miners can remember the good days of transport. There is no longer a British lorry manufactured in this country and with ever in-creasing rules and regulations there will not be any British drivers in a few years' time either. I was on the M40 recently coming home from a show in the Midlands with 373 FOD and was constantly passed by foreign lorries with un-pronounceable names written on them…

…How can it all have gone so horribly wrong??

Chapter Twelve

BRIAN HARRIS 1943 TO 2012

Since the second edition of this book in 2007 Brian continued to run Brian Harris Transport Limited as a clearing house and he ran a couple of pick-ups with tri-axle trailers up and down the country. He still had Fine Tubes, Plymouth, as a customer and he used two or three of his ex-drivers as and when needed. He would also drive one himself from time to time. So life for him carried on much the same way but without the worry of running a fleet of lorries. He was doing what he had always done but now with some spare time. He bought himself a new Range Rover which he promptly put through a car wash with the back window partly open! Gary Ball, responsible for washing and valeting the car, rebuked him severely but Brian, in his own lovely way, replied "I'll get another one!"

So life settled into a routine and the pick-ups brought in the beer money! Ex-drivers Keith Winters and Brian Newbury were two that kept the wheels turning but then legislation reared its ugly head once again and the pick-ups now needed digital tachographs and drivers equipped with 'digi cards'. Good friend of mine, Edward Goodwin, had just retired from long distance driving and was a regular drinking buddy of Brian at the Rugglestone and he had an up to date card. So he drove the pick-ups and was the last one to do so before Brian died. On one such trip to Scotland Brian rang him and asked Edward to go over to Ayrshire to load a motorbike into the trailer and bring it back to Devon for a customer; this was extra to what was originally asked of Edward. On his return he met Brian in the Rugglestone who pressed some folding money into Ed's pocket with the comment "I made good money out of that job so here's some of it for you." As Edward said to me; he was in Scotland anyway so it should just have been part of the job.

After his mother Margaret died in November 2008 Brian now had to cope on his own which did not come easy. He had never fended for himself and I think it had a lasting effect on him but friends rallied round and life for Brian continued with a manageable routine; boiled eggs for dinner on a Thursday!

It was at this time that life-long friends Gerald and Christine Lamb became a great comfort to him. Christine is from the Miners family and although no blood relative to Brian she was extremely close to him and took over the roll as Company secretary and generally kept things on an even keel. She and Gerald persuaded Brian to go on holiday, go and visit Scotland, go off to classic truck shows where Gary and I would take the KV, and enjoy the Range Rover. He forever said he could never get away because of business or his mother but all that had (sadly) changed. He was warming to the idea but unfortunately none of it came to pass as Brian was taken ill and after a short spell in Torbay Hospital; he passed away on the third of April 2012.

I think it fair to say that Brian's affairs were possibly not as tidy as they could be; especially as he died with no descendants. A firm of solicitors in Torquay now had the job of sorting everything out. A lot of which could have been avoided and could have saved a lot of expense from his estate. Christine now had to deal with it and one of her very first tasks was to ask Gary and me for the keys to the KV. The whole yard was in complete lock-down immediately after his death. Christine was not even allowed to release the lorry to be used to carry Brian to his funeral and he was brought to the church in what I can best describe as a glorified Mercedes Sprinter van. There were many raised eyebrows over that but poor Christine's hands were well and truly tied!

So it was that on Saturday 14th April at noon, 600 people gathered together at St. Pancras Church, Widecombe-in-the-Moor to attend the funeral of Brian Harris. Standing room only and many standing outside. The transport industry turned out in force from all over the UK to pay their last respects. I think all his ex-employees that were able to be there were there and seven of them, plus Derek Greenaway of Cannon Commercials, were pallbearers; he was a big man! I was honoured to have been asked to give a tribute to Brian at the Church; and so it was that I stood trembling in front of 600 people. I think it went OK as I managed to lighten the tone and got them laughing.

A lovely tribute to Brian was the appearance of the two preserved ERF artic units that are on the road and in his colours. F513 MOD, owned by Gary Ball, and D345 OTT, owned by Clint Moorey, were positioned at the top of Widecombe Hill looking down onto the Church in the valley below with Union Jack flags flying. Everyone attending the funeral would have come past them on their way to Widecombe. In the absence of the KV it was a fitting gesture and thanks must go to Gary and Clint; especially to Clint for bringing his lorry all the way from Kent.

After the service he was buried in the churchyard next to his parents and the Church clock now has four faces on the tower thanks to the generosity of Brian. We then made our way down the hill to the Rugglestone Inn where the landlord, Richard and his staff, laid on a pig roast in the beer garden. Luckily under a marquee as just as proceedings were getting under way there was one almighty clap of thunder followed by a short cloud burst; almost as if Brian was having the last word!

AND FINALLY

The following piece was penned by me for the REVS Magazine (Register of ERF Vehicles Society of which Brian was a member) shortly after his funeral.

Brian Harris was born on the 6th September 1943 and as soon as he left school he joined the family business of Harris & Miners Transport. A specially built lightweight Thames Trader was ordered for him so he could get on the road before he was 21. In 1966 his father, Jerry, took him off the road and gave him the office to run. This he did until Jerry died in 1978 when Brian gained sole control of the Company which then changed name to Brian Harris Transport Ltd. Thus it remained until closure in 2000.

His death marks the end of an era in the transport world. There were few like him, a real character and much respected in the industry as was evident at the funeral on April the 14th at Widecombe-in-the-Moor Parish Church. 600 people turned up to pay their respects from all over the country; I was privileged to have been asked to do a eulogy at the service.

A no frills man, a transport man through and through who was not afraid to get his hands dirty and a man who ran over 30 lorries (predominately ERFs) virtually single handed from a little office in the corner of the yard in Bovey Tracey. On the road was a distinctive and proud fleet seen up and down the country from Devon to Scotland but the yard came a poor second. Water would often flood his office as it was next to the lorry wash but Brian's answer to that was that he was not asking anyone else to sit in it! The remedy was to prop his chair up on a pallet to rise above the tide!

He loved a pint or two with his drivers at the end of the week when all was forgiven as he was quite prone to hiring and firing you on the same day and then hiring you again amongst an outpouring of very choice language! A very generous man whose only luxury in life was a new Jaguar every 3 years or so; and then he would lend it to a driver or fitter to go off on holiday. He seldom had a day off himself, let alone a holiday.

After the Company closed Brian had the first ERF bought by Harris & Miners in 1960 rebuilt over 3 years. He became a member of the Register of ERF Vehicles Society (REVS) and from 2005 the Gardner engine KV was seen attending many rallies and road-runs. I was extremely privileged to have been one of his ex- drivers to take that lorry to many events including the 75th Anniversary of ERF in 2008 at Chester.

Characters like Brian Harris are rarely encountered and he will be greatly missed among the haulage industry and those involved with the preservation of classic lorries. I can only hope we will see the KV ERF about again as Brian had no immediate family and as I write this tribute to him the future of it is unknown.

Another picture of OOD 504M driven by Maurice Gouldthorpe who started in the quarry before 'going on the road' as a driver. These 240 Gardner powered ERFs were the backbone of the fleet in the 1970s. (Photo: Allen Taylor).

Lisa Ritson with her grandfather, Maurice Gouldthorpe, on one of her trips with him. Quite often drivers would take their children/grandchildren with them. Not many firms would allow this today; 'elf 'n safety! (Photo: Lisa Ritson).

An early picture of Gordon Bamsey on his first 'stint' for Harris & Miners; he then went on to drive for Hottot Transport before returning to Brian Harris and remained with him until after the auction. GUO 847D was Cummins powered. (Photo: Barry Rowe)

DV 686N 'Peter Davey' newly painted and fitted with a Jennings sleeper conversion, ready to go back on the road in August 1981. While Jerry was alive he would not have sleeper cabs on the fleet. However, after he died in 1978 it gradually got converted. Bit of a shelf on the A Series ERFs, like this one, as the only method of getting into the driver's bunk was by cutting off the back of the passenger seat! Just think about it... by 1981 the Swedes were importing to this country Volvo 88s and Scania 111s, and had been doing so for several years. (Photo: Dave Godley)

2010 Heart of Wales Run at the Ponderosa Café on the top of the Horseshoe Pass. Gary and I took the KV on this two day run for classic commercial vehicles. Another KV, this one an artic unit, comes past the Harris & Miners KV parked up for a coffee stop. (Photo: the author)

Shrewsbury cattle market September 2010 at the start of the Heart of Wales Run. (Photo: the author)

June 2006 Gaydon at the Classic and Vintage Commercial Show. Gary used his unit 'Monarch of the Moor' to carry our Leyland Octopus, of 1949 vintage, to the event while I drove the Harris & Miners KV there. As the Octopus is the slowest it made sense to carry it; her top speed is 28mph.(Photos: Dave Gothard)

Gaydon 2011. Truck Model World's class winner and best in show; beating competition from all over the country. The picture belongs to the builder of this 1/24th scale model of the Guy Big J that the author drove in 1975/6. It has to be seen to be believed and John is now the very proud owner of it. (Photo: Andy Lee)

Another model of the fleet by Andy Lee. (Photo: Andy Lee)

This time one of the blue fleet modelled by Andy Lee. Gordon Bamsey, the driver of the lorry of which this is the model, stands beside Brian for a picture taken by Tara Newman.

C149 JOD 'Moorland Eagle' seen on the M5 near Gordano. A Gardner engine drop-side 8 legged tipper of which Brian had several over the years. Jimmy Webster had this one new in 1986 and when it was replaced by G496 WDV it was sold to Martin Bowring. (Photo: Barrie John Robert Baker)

D204 PDV. A 290 Cummins engine drop-sided tipper seen here at Tuckers Maltings in Newton Abbot. No pictures of this 8 legger appear in previous editions of this book. After service with Brian Harris it was sold to Simpsons and converted to timber haulage. It is now in a sorry state but survives (just) at Exbourne, near Okehampton. (Photo: Allan Bedford)

Another shot of D204 PDV taken by Michael Marshall

C149 JOD. Now in Martin Bowring colours at Allaston Grove Sawmills, Lydney, Gloucestershire. 'Elf 'n Safety would have a fit today if they saw timber loaded across a lorry (Photo: Martin Perry).

Christmas Eve 1981. Before we all went to the pub on Christmas Eve Brian always liked to have two of the fleet parked outside his office for all to see over the holiday. A rare picture of the one and only Foden that was in Harris & Miners colours. A 240 Gardner engined S80 that was new to Reg Hill. The author drove it briefly before Jimmy Webster then took it on. (Photo: Dave Godley)

No picture of this S80 Foden was found for the first or second edition of this book so it is a bonus that this one has turned up. Location and date unknown but now with a sleeper pod fitted. (Photo: Bill Reid)

September 2015 Cribbs Causeway, Bristol. Gary Ball stops here overnight en route to the start of the Heart of Wales Run. This year he decided to trailer the KV to the event behind his E Series which itself is not yet old enough to enter as all the lorries have to be at least 30 years old. (Photo: Gary Ball)

A rare picture of one of the many Ford Transit trucks that came and went; and rusted away! Even the smallest vehicle on the fleet was turned out in full company colours and this is another one signwritten by the Author. (Photo: Marcus Lester)

April 14th 2012. 'Monarch of the Moor' owned by Gary Ball and 'Daniel Whiddon' owned by Clint Moorey look down Widecombe Hill to Widecombe Church. A fitting tribute for everyone that came to the funeral to see. Clint brought his ERF from Kent to be alongside Gary's ERF that lives locally. (Photo: Clint Moorey)

The two preserved ERFs look down Widecombe Hill to the Church in Widecombe-in-the-Moor on a grey and sad day in April 2012. They were so positioned that everyone attending Brian's funeral would have driven past. As the KV 'Happy Wanderer' could not be used (the solicitors would not release it) this was a lovely tribute. Thanks must go to Gary Ball and Clint Moorey for organising it. (Photo: Ian Ashby)

(Photo: Ian Ashby)

Very few drivers would carry a camera with them but Michael Bartholomew (Bart) did. Here he is stuck at junction 40 of the M6 for two days waiting to deliver to Keswick Pencil Company. (Photo: Michael Bartholomew)

Bart stops to snap this lovely picture which epitomises the work Brian did; a variety of loads from Devon and Cornwall to the North of Scotland. This time bins from Dartmouth (where Bart lives) to Perth. (Photo: Michael Bartholomew)

Bart stops to take this picture as he makes his way out onto the A7 near Galashiels; presumably to load as the trailer is empty. (Photo: Michael Bartholomew)

Fine Tubes, Estover, Plymouth 2001. Bart poses beside P680 YTT, 'Dartmoor Lassie', with the specially made steel carrying trailer that went to Parsons Transport (along with the job) at the closing down auction just a few months after this picture was taken. The unit went into preservation and was bought by Peter Wright to pull a low-loader to transport his Burrel Showmans tractor. It has subsequently been sold and now resides somewhere in the North East of England in a sorry state. The names on the lorries were used more than once as the Author drove an A Series ERF back in the '70s bearing the name 'Dartmoor Lassie'. (Photo: Michael Bartholomew)

D204 PDV. This picture was taken on Christmas Eve 2015 and clearly shows the sad state of this 8 legger. After leaving the service of Brian Harris Transport it went to Simpsons on timber haulage with the tipper body removed and a crane fitted. The crane has now been disposed of and the lorry rests in a yard at Exbourne, near Okehampton. In the words of Steve Cockerham, who kindly took the picture, "it would take a brave man to restore that". Not impossible though, the running gear is probably quite serviceable and the engine is preserved (if it still has an engine) under what remains of the cab. Another cab will be available somewhere and a new body can easily be built. Two ingredients are necessary; knowledge and money. (Photo: Steve Cockerham)

An inside the cab view of D204 POD on Christmas Eve 2015. (Photo: Steve Cockerham)

Chapter Thirteen

THE AUCTION OF THE 'HAPPY WANDERER'

Following the funeral of Brian Harris in April 2012 the fate of the ERF KV 373 FOD 'Happy Wanderer', or 'Old Faithful' as she was affectionately known, became a concern. Gary Ball and I had taken her to various shows up and down the country since the completion of the rebuild in 2005. Now the lorry was out of bounds to us and locked away in the shed at the back of the yard; the KV was now part of Brian's estate and like his other vehicles were assets to be disposed of. The Range Rover, pick-ups and trailers had already gone and as the KV was not mentioned in a will so it too was to be sold.

The executors of Brian's estate refused an offer from Gary and they also refused an offer of a considerable amount from a local haulier in Kingsteignton, Newton Abbot. £23,000 to be precise. Their reasoning being that the lorry had to go to auction to gain the best price. The best price was certainly got but not for the executors! They had completely misjudged the whole situation and shot themselves in the foot. So, on Thursday 20th September 2012 the lorry went to auction at DVCA Auctions held near Wincanton in Somerset. Up until this time the lorry had not been seen out during 2012 but left neglected, and out of test, awaiting an uncertain future.

By this time Gary had got a syndicate together and hopefully bid for the lorry at the auction. Life-long friends Gerald and Christine Lamb, ex Brian Harris driver Bryn Jones, Derek Greenaway of Cannon Commercials and Gary. I am not part of the syndicate as I have an interest in three other preserved lorries that keep me busy; and a daughter's wedding to pay for that kept me poor! However, I did do the bidding on their behalf. Edward Goodwin, Gary Ball and myself were at the auction and dear Gary, bless him, got so worried about losing the lorry that he really was not up to doing the bidding so Edward suggested I do it and I ended up with the buyer's number.

So there we were observing people looking at the lorry prior to the start of the auction and listening to their remarks. One comment that came up several times was that the MOT was out of date. We knew that it would easily pass but would-be buyers did not; so that was our little secret! There was a lot of interest shown in the KV and when the time came for lot number 277 to go under the hammer the auctioneer certainly gave the lorry a good build up. "The subject of a £35,000 nut and bolt restoration and being sold as part of a deceased estate."

"Will someone start the bidding at £10,000?"

I came in at £11,250 which was quickly topped at £11,500. Back in I go at £11,750 and what happened next was staggering. In fact nothing happened and the hammer went down on my bid of £11,750!! Including buyer's premium and VAT the total came to £13,633.76p. What a result, we all expected to be paying a lot more than that. In fact, the worry was running out of what the syndicate could muster and losing the lorry that way. There was, however, a generous haulier from Somerset present who knew Brian and said to us to keep going with the bidding and he would make up the shortfall. He really did not want that lorry to go anywhere else. As it turned out we did not need his kind offer of help. Much since has been said about the low price realised for such an iconic lorry. Obviously letting the test run out was not a good idea and that particular auction was mostly cars. Had a bigger up-country auction been chosen that specialised in classic lorries then there could have been a very different outcome. However, it could not have been a better result for the syndicate and great news for anyone interested in Brian Harris Transport.

Personally, I have many fond memories of 'Happy Wanderer' going back to my early days as a driver for Harris & Miners. Before getting 'my own' lorry and whilst on holiday relief I drove the KV for a few weeks in 1975 when Dick Barrs, the regular and practically only driver of that lorry, was on holiday. Gary drove her at the funeral of Ted Butt and as already written he should have been doing the same for Brian's funeral. In the years between the rebuild completed in 2005 and Brian's passing I was one of the lucky ones to drive her to many events; including the 75th anniversary rally of ERF held near Chester where I met Peter Foden.

The next day Cannon Commercials collected 'Old Faithful' and returned her to her rightful home in Devon. As the MOT was out of date Cannon Commercials also got the job of delivering her to the auction on behalf of the executors. After selling fees, VAT and cost of getting the lorry to Wincanton they would not have cleared £10,000.

She now shares a shed not far from Bovey Tracey with Gary's own ex Brian Harris ERF 'E' Series and our own Taunton Cider Leyland Octopus.

A rear view of D204 PDV in happier times. (Photo: Allan Bedford)

The KV passing Widecombe Church, driven by the author, on a freezing day in March 2013 on a photo shoot for a magazine. The clock faces were donated by the Harris family. (Photo: Gyles Carpenter)

March 2013 outside Widecombe Church. The three preserved ERFs that are currently running are gathered together for a magazine photo shoot that was featured in Heritage Commercials in August 2013. The article was penned by Alan Barnes who also took this picture.

March 2013 outside the Cromwell Arms in Bovey Tracey, one of Brian's watering holes. A pity this picture was taken before the pub opened as the Author was driving the Harris & Miners KV on a freezing cold day with no heater. He could have done with something to have warmed him up! (Photo: Alan Barnes)

Photo shoot March 2013. Two ex-drivers, Gary Ball and the Author, stand outside the Pottery Road yard with the sign that once stood proudly on posts at the entrance to the yard. (Photo: Alan Barnes)

D345 OTT making its way to Brian's local, March 2013. The Author signwrote both the lorry and the sign! (Photo: Alan Barnes)

Brian in his favourite seat at the Rugglestone Inn shortly before his sudden illness. Quite possibly the last picture ever taken of him. (Photo: Christine Lamb)

'Dartmoor Avenger' T470 AFJ in South Molton. Another previously unseen picture of the last new ERF on the fleet. New in 1999 and as Lot number 164 made £20,000 at the auction on April the 18th 2001. (Photo: Allen Taylor)

T470 AFJ bought by Kelvedon Transport Co. Ltd., of Newport, South Wales. Subsequently seen at a Dealers in the Midlands and now owned by Malcolm Gray who is returning it to the original colours and it will remain in preservation; a bit of good news there as it had been badly treated, especially the interior. (Photo: Clint Moorey)

T470 AFJ being transported on the back of the Atki owned by Paul Trickey, a friend of Malcolm Gray who now owns the ERF. It can clearly be seen how the lorry has deteriorated. (Photo: Malcolm Gray)

T470 AFJ with donor vehicle from Andrew Meer. The plan was to recab T470 but the new idea is to retain the original cab and change the interior trim from the good trim of the donor vehicle. (Photo: Malcolm Gray)

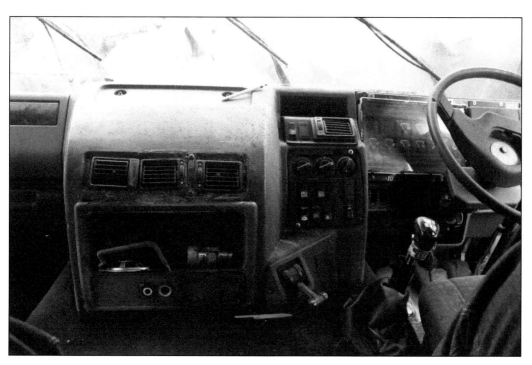

The trashed interior of T470 AFJ. This is what Malcolm Gray has bought and why it was necessary to buy a donor vehicle with a good interior trim. How has it been allowed to get in this state? (Photo: Malcolm Gray)

Oh dear! (Photo: Malcolm Gray)

F762 KOD is now owned by Jon Prowse and awaits further restoration after being allowed to weather badly left outside on the Lizard in Cornwall by a previous owner. (Photo: Andy Lee)

F762 KOD awaits further restoration in a barn in the Teign Valley in Devon. One day it is hoped it will join the other preserved ones on the rally scene. (Photo: Jon Prowse)

KSU 762V 'Widecombe Warrior' was bought second hand from good friends of Brian Harris; Reeve and Grossart of Abington. It is pictured in the first edition of this book still in Reeve and Grossart livery and with a 33ft trailer behind it loading clay at Longcliffe in 1983. A year later it is again pictured in the first edition but now all light blue in Brian Harris livery and here it is in this edition in the proper livery of the 'blue fleet'. The Author remembers being given strict instructions to retain the thistle emblem when he did the signwriting.

D345 OTT in its working clothes when part of the 'blue fleet' and now in preservation living in Kent and owned by Clint Moorey. (Photo: Clint Moorey)

'Tom Pearce' resting in the yard at Pottery Road for some reason missing its number plate. It is N155 TDV which was new in 1995 and fetched £5,500 six years later at the auction. Used on the Brian Harris calendar 1999. (Photo: Andy Lee)

Yer Tiz was the name Gerry Snell used when he drove this ERF on Westmac Machinery. (Photo: Steve Wilkinson)

RFJ 859W 'Harry Hawke' in the yard April 1985 with a familiar mixed load for here, there and everywhere! Peter Rees had this M Series ERF from new. Still in Harris & Miners livery but with a Brian Harris headboard as after 1978 the Company changed its name as Brian gained control. The headboards were the first visible signs. This lorry has sliding door glass as can be seen on the driver's door; unusual as the other M Series on the fleet had drop down windows. (Photo: Dave Godley)

A line up of ERFs and one Leyland in the yard in April 1985. Note the blue curtain-sider trailer second from the right; early days for the Company to start using curtain-siders. (Photo: Dave Godley)

The Pottery Road yard on November 20th 2015. A sad sight with neglected buildings and a far cry from happier times. (Photo: the Author)

In chapter five of the book the Author told the story of how the only Seddon appeared on the fleet but no picture of it was ever found to include in the first two editions. Then, with only days to go before the completed third edition went off to the publishers, this one was sent by Dave Godley. Taken at the end of its working life in 1985 and parked on the ramp so it could be bump started while being used as the yard shunter. Already minus the mirrors and no longer taxed but showing the Jennings sleeper addition more commonly seen on the A Series ERFs. When this lorry was new dealers were selling them off at a knock down price as the more observant reader will have noticed that it is a P reg. By then Seddon had taken over Atkinson and the new Seddon Atkinson 400 Series was available from 1975; also P reg. It was already out of date before it even went on the road; also in 1975. The 'Grey Mare' was new to Jimmy Webster. The Author also had a brief spell driving it after Jimmy had moved on to another lorry. (Photo: Dave Godley)

Thursday 20th September 2012, DVCA Auction, Templecombe, Somerset. Lot 277 (number in windscreen) awaits an uncertain future. Despite the best efforts of the auctioneer the estimate was not met and the hammer went down at £11,750 to the syndicate from Devon. The 'Happy Wanderer' needs to wander no more and is in safe hands. (Photo: the Author)

HTA 742D 'Devon Pixie' being loaded in the yard on the 12th August 1981. Brian Harris on the headboard but original Harris & Miners livery on the cab. The lorry the Author took to the Republic of Ireland on several trips in 1975/6. (Photo: Dave Godley)

Just been delivered to the yard and ready to go on the road. Not yet registered and no number plates fitted but it will be CFJ 951T. Supplied by Frank Tucker of Exeter and body by Bovey Commercials, just down the road from the yard. Fitted with a drop-side body and greedy boards. Interestingly although the year is 1979 the livery is still Harris & Miners but with Brian Harris on the headboard. Brian gained control of the business in 1978 following the death of his father that year. (Photo: Dave Godley)

NOD 160P 'Widecombe Lad' pictured in the yard on the 20th August 1981. This lorry is pictured again (at Michaelwood services) on the 14th June 1982 but now with a Jennings sleeper conversion. The 8 wheel tippers on the fleet were very much 'distance motors'. (Photo: Dave Godley)

G901 STA 'Dartmoor Lady' was new to 'Jock' Phil Wilde. Seen here pulling the step-frame trailer. (Photo: Barrie John Robert Baker)

Chapter Fourteen

WHERE ARE THEY NOW?
AN UPDATE OF THE PRESERVED LORRIES ONCE ON THE FLEET

This is the final say on the history of the Company unless someone pens an article for one of the magazines specialising in classic lorries and road transport.

Such is the following for Brian Harris Transport that although much has been written in the past just maybe that will happen. There are two known ERFs once part of the fleet that are in the throes of being restored and a third gently rotting in a field near Okehampton that is unlikely ever to see the road again. A fourth one is in a bad shape somewhere in the North East of the country. P680 YTT, an ERF EC14, once driven by Jerry Snell, did make it into preservation and was used by its owner to pull his Burrell Showman's tractor on a Taskers trailer; smartly turned out retaining the Brian Harris livery. Since then things have gone badly downhill and the future is uncertain. There is also a Commer that not that many months ago left a barn near Taunton where it had rested for many years and now has a new home. The Thames Trader that sold at the closing down sale in 2001 is also still ongoing as a restoration project.

Three ERFs are very much on the 'preservation scene' and have been together again this year on the Devon Coastal Run held on July 18th. Only one of them bears the Harris & Miners livery, the KV 'Happy Wanderer', so if the Commer and Thames Trader, owned by Graham Orchard, remain in their original colours when restored there could be three. Out of the three regularly seen out and about D345 OTT, owned by Clint Moorey from Strood in Kent, remains the only one in the blue livery; quite possibly always to be the only blue one.

The two ERFs in the process of restoration both have interesting histories. F762 KOD has left the Lizard peninsula, as reported in the second edition, and is safe in the hands of Jon Prowse in his barn in the Teign Valley. New cab floor and door pillars have been fitted and in the words of Jon "awaiting further restoration by me or someone else". Chris Sawford bought this one at the closure auction and always rated it as a good lorry. When he asked Brian which one to buy he was told 'Phantom of the Moor' was the one to go for. Unfortunately it was the next owner that left it to rot out in the open, facing the Atlantic Ocean on the Lizard. Gary Ball had a hand in fetching it back with his own unit 'Monarch of the Moor'.

The other one, T470 AFJ 'Dartmoor Avenger', was the very last new one to be bought by Brian and was only two years old when sold at the closure auction. It was coupled to a new 26 pallet 45 foot trailer and driven by Derek Ellis 'Del Boy'. It is also the first one to be modelled by Corgi. Now owned by Malcolm Gray, it is being restored to its former glory. Originally the plan was to recab it from a donor vehicle obtained from Andrew Meer as the interior was in poor shape. How it got like it during the years with Kelvedon Transport is not known. However, the plan is now to retain the original cab and tranship the interior. From the pictures Malcolm has sent to me it is in a terrible state. How a lorry can be allowed to deteriorate like that beggars belief; especially as it is barely sixteen years old. Luckily it is now in safe hands and will once again be in BH livery.

Other than those, Gary Ball knew of an ex Brian Harris ERF E10 shunting in Maningtree Docks, Essex. It was privately owned on loan to, or working for, the docks. Gary has not been in those docks for three or more years so its present whereabouts are unknown.

The three that are restored have regularly been seen at events up and down the country since last reported on in the second edition. In 2006 Gary and I took three lorries to the classic truck show at Gaydon. Quite a weekend and one worth mentioning here. Gary put the idea into my head to take the then newly refurbished and repainted Taunton Cider Octopus. He carried it behind his ERF and I drove the KV. I set off well before Gary, as the KV is a lot slower, and with a good friend of mine, Vic McCarthy, we arrived at Stow on the Wold at about 10pm having gone far enough for the day. We had left Bovey Tracey at 5pm. Five hours was enough and we needed a pint! I pulled into Tesco's car park and a very nice security man said we could park up for the night in a faraway corner of it.

It was one of those barmy summer's nights; warm and starlit. After a pint or three in the town, Vic and I rolled out our sleeping bags on the back of the KV; the only disturbance was Gary turning up at 2 in the morning!

Gaydon was reached by 9 o'clock and we left Gary busy polishing the E14 and KV after we had unloaded the tanker and parked up. Vic and I had a good day looking at all the exhibits, including a fantastic display of model trucks in the conference suite upstairs above the Heritage Motor Centre. The beer tent was visited on occasions and Gary checked up on, still polishing away! He appeared at the beer tent, absolutely filthy, at 10 o'clock that evening after spending thirteen hours cleaning and polishing. The next day the KV won best in class in the concours event and one of the judges said to me "I suppose you will be driving it back to Devon after he has done all that work to win the prize and you have stood in the beer tent watching him?" "Yes."

In 2008 Gary and I drove the KV all the way to Kelsall, near Chester, for the 75th anniversary celebrations of ERF. Over 200 ERFs gathered together in one place and Peter Foden was the guest of honour being chauffeured around the rally site in his Bentley registered ERF 1. Sadly we have since lost Edwin Peter Foden CBE (he died in 2012) but it was wonderful to meet him. A long way to drive that lorry but an event well worth the effort and an amusing incident occurred on the way home.

On the way down the A49 on the Monday morning following the rally we stopped at a vintage caravan snack wagon near Ludlow when a posh Mercedes car pulled in and the occupant, all suited and booted, came in and enquired of the proprietor behind the counter who was with the Harris & Miners ERF and we were pointed out to him. Over he came and asked if we knew anything about the book written about the Company to which Gary replied "this is the man who wrote it" as he looked at me. His face was a picture but there was better to come. It just so happened I had a spare copy in the cab that I could sell him and sign it as well! He went away happy.

One other event worth mentioning was a freezing day in March 2013 when the three preserved lorries, once part of the fleet, were assembled for a photo shoot for a forthcoming article in Heritage Commercials written by Alan Barnes. He and Gyles Carpenter, well known truck photographer, came to Devon to take many pictures in various locations around Bovey Tracey, on Dartmoor, and in Widecombe-in-the-Moor. It was published in the August edition of that year.

Clint Moorey came down from Kent with D345 OTT, Daniel Whiddon, to join Gary's F513 MOD, 'Monarch of the Moor', and 373 FOD, 'Happy Wanderer'. I was asked if I would like to drive the KV for the day, an opportunity not to be missed and I was pleased to do it. One snag, it was probably the coldest day of the year so far and I am spending it driving around Dartmoor in a lorry with no heater. I spent the whole time freezing and watching the other two swanning around in cabs like saunas!

On the weekend of the Devon Coastal Run in July 2012 I met Andy Lee who had come to the event to show me a model he had made of the Harris & Miners Guy Big J, XUO 389K, 'Peter Gurney', the lorry I drove having taken it over from Ted Butt who had it when new. It is a fantastic 1/24th scale model correct in every detail and copied from the cover photograph of the first two editions of this book; only Skipper the dog is missing! Even my map book is on the dash. The trailer has every knot on the sheeted load in exactly the same place as in the picture. In 2011 Andy won best in show at the Truck Model World exhibition at the Heritage Motor Centre at Gaydon; the biggest model truck show in the country. It was subsequently pictured on the cover of the TMW magazine in October 2011. Andy does not sell his models, or build to order, so I never thought it would one day come my way. However, on October the 4th 2015 it was given to me by my family on my 70th birthday. For that I shall be eternally grateful to them and Andy. He has built several models of the Harris & Miners/Brian Harris fleet and is currently working on a model of one of the many Commers to bear the livery.

The final chapter has now been reached in the continuing story of this unique Company that was well respected throughout its life. How many small haulage firms have had so much written about them in so many magazines and how many firms, big or small, have had so many Corgi models made of their fleet? Not many. Let's hope that the owners of the preserved lorries once part of the fleet will be able to show them for years to come and keep the name alive.

John Corah.

S690 BTA pictured new in 1998 in Mill Marsh Park, Bovey Tracey. The Historic Transport Club's annual show on the third Sunday in July. The Author is the Rally Secretary of the Club and in this year a collection of new lorries were gathered together to be seen alongside the many classic ones on show. Next to this one can be seen a Leyland Daf belonging to Ken Thomas Transport who brought three classic lorries to the event. Ken Thomas Transport is another haulage firm sadly no longer operating. (Photo: Allan Bedford)

P680 YTT 'Dartmoor Lassie' at the Royal Cornwall Show in June 1996. It was quite a regular thing for Brian to have a new lorry on the stand of the ERF agents, Tuckers of Exeter. (Photo: Barrie John Robert Baker)

DTA 279L was another lorry to bear the name 'Dartmoor Lassie'. A rather grainy picture, but the only one available, of this 240 Gardner powered A Series ERF now sporting a Jennings sleeper cab conversion. This was the Author's lorry after Reg Hill had it when new. Seen here loading clay at Lee Mill near Plymouth. (Photo: John Corah)

1995 Bournemouth to Bath Run on the first Sunday in September; morning coffee stop in Salisbury. Every year throughout the 1990s the Author borrowed a unit and step frame trailer to carry the Taunton Cider Leyland Octopus which he shares with fellow Historic Transport Club members, Phil Day and Edward Goodwin. The Octopus would do the Run under its own power and then be picked up from Bath to be taken back to Bovey Tracey. (Photo: John Corah)

Another 1990s Bournemouth to Bath Run, not sure of the exact year. Lunchtime stop at the Royal Oak, near Longleat, on the way to the finish in Bath . This time borrowing an ERF E14 for the weekend. Edward Goodwin's landrover gets a lift to Bath. It is needed as four people cannot get in Brian's ERF on the way to Bournemouth or back home from Bath; but on the Sunday Run there are seats for all as the Octopus is doing the Run. All 90 miles of it at a top speed of 28mph! A good reason for carrying it to Bournemouth or we would never make the pub before closing time! (Photo: John Corah)

Spares department, Pottery Road Depot. (Photo: John Henderson)

Spares department, Pottery Road Depot. The green ERF was bought in as a yard shunter as the present yard shunter was part-exed for this one. However, this one had a bit of test left on it so it was pressed into service until it ran out.
(Photo: John Corah)

F516 MOD on Chudleigh bank. A load from Western Machinery at Ivybridge, a firm no longer with us.
(Photo: Martin Perry)

D204 PDV en route to Crief on the M5 driven by Pat McKenna. (Photo: Marcus Lester)

Gary Ball with his own ex Brian Harris E14 carrying the KV he has a share in to a show. The E14 is the unit he drove for Brian Harris from joining the Company in January 1990 until closure and then bought it at the auction in April 2001. He still has it 26 years on. (Photo: Ian Ashby)

F380 HFJ 'Uncle' was new to Peter Rees. Uncle being the name of Brian and Margaret's dog. When the sheets were new you could recognise one of these lorries way in the distance. Peter's name can also be seen written on the cab step; a custom adopted on all of the lorries and whenever they came up for painting and signwriting the Author had to find out whose lorry it was and what name was wanted on the step. (Photo: Nigel Parkin)

D932 POD was new to Reg Hill in 1996. On two occasions in the 1990s Reg took the Taunton Cider Leyland Octopus, on the step frame trailer, to a rally at the steam railway on the Isle of Wight. Here is his unit parked up for the weekend while he and Ron Westaway, who went with him, went off to the pub.(Photo: Bill Reid)

P150 EFL 'Dartmoor Crusader' was bought second hand and is seen here on the M5 showing off the Authors signwriting on the unit and trailer. The colour scheme on the cab was the final design used with the light green top half. (Photo: Ian Ashby)

D345 OTT 'Daniel Whiddon' now in preservation and owned by Clint Moorey from Kent. Seen here at a truck show at Gaydon in 2015 carrying his father's Atkinson. (Photo: Clint Moorey)

Brian Harris in the Welcome Stranger in the days when Pat and Margaret McKenna ran the pub in the 1980s before Pat joined Brian as a driver. (Photo: Tina Rowe)

JTA 505E 'Moorland Princess' went on to give many years' service on the fairground circuit after being disposed of by Brian Harris. Now fitted with a box body that came from Hush Puppies. This was the Author's lorry before going on to an artic… the Big J. (Photo: John Corah)

XUO 389K 'Peter Gurney' was new to Ted Butt and then passed on to the Author who now owns the 1/24th scale model of it made by Andy Lee. The only Guy Big J on the fleet. (Photo: John Corah)

John Corah's 70th birthday at the Dolphin Hotel in Bovey Tracey with family and friends, where he was presented with this magnificent model of the Guy Big J and sheeted load. (Photo: The Author)

A773 NFJ was the first of two Leyland Road Trains to be bought by Brian Harris and both were driven by Billy Baty who loved the room in the cab compared to the lack of it in an ERF. Pictured on the M5 near Gordano. (Photo: Barrie John Robert Baker)

BTT 392Y on the M5 near Gordano. Many pictures in these sort of publications are taken at static locations so it is nice to be able to include some photos of the fleet on the move. (Photo: Barrie John Robert Baker)

F762 KOD 'Phantom of the Moor', one of the F reg units that went for £1,000 at the auction seen here on the M5 near Gordano with paper. Must be fine weather as the load is only fly sheeted. (Photo: Barrie John Robert Baker)

D204 PDV in Simpsons' yard and in their colours. The crane has since been removed and the lorry is in need of a little TLC! (Photo: James Simpson)

N169 TFJ 'Uncle' on Dixtons roundabout, Monmouth. (Photo: Martin Perry)

'Dan'l Whiddon' a 1966 Commer that was sold on to a farmer and survives. This picture was taken in 2015 on a farm near Taunton where it has been kept for many years. Recently found a new home and it is hoped it will be restored and kept in its original colours. (Photo: Ian 'Snowy' Cullen)

A lovely shot of 'The Monarch' and 'Happy Wanderer' on the 2010 Devon Coastal Run in Bovey Tracey. The Author's eldest daughter, Katie, took the picture and she also helped to sort out all the pictures in this book. John's computer expertise leaves something to be desired! (Photo: Katie Sandford)

The entrance to the yard. I remember taking the picture myself not long after the new sign that I made and signwrote was put up at the entrance. (Photo: John Corah)

John Liddicoat took this lovely picture on a trip he made with D257 STA, ERF 'Tom Pearce' in 1987. The setting is Eilean Donnan Castle, Dornie, on the west coast of Scotland. The boat had been picked up from Honner Marine of Totnes, South Devon, and was destined for the Orkney Isles. John took it as far as Scrabster, just 14 miles from John O'Groats. This picture and the picture below was originally displayed on the back cover of the first and second editions of the book. (Photo: John Liddicoat)

A frosty winter's night in Leith in 1988. Note the frost line on the diesel tank caused by warm diesel returning to the tank from the engine, as is the practice with Cummins units. Loaded with farm machinery from Western Machinery of Ivybridge in South Devon. Derek "Soapy" Hudson is captured adjusting his television picture for an evening in! It was his first trip with this new lorry. (Photo: Joe Donaldson from John Henderson collection)

This photo was originally on the front cover of the first and second editions of the book. It shows Guy Big J, XUO 389K, 'Peter Gurney' poses for the camera with "John the Dog" and Skipper; his trusty travelling companion. Yes, it is the author in thinner and hairier mode in 1976. He took this lorry on from Ted Butt, who had it new in 1972, after giving up the 4-wheeler Albion. The load is 20 tons of Spanboard from South Molton, all sheeted and roped ready to leave the depot in Bovey Tracey for Glasgow. This was the only Guy on the fleet and a most reliable, if a little slow, lorry. Powered by a very smooth Gardner 6LXB '180' engine and a 6-speed Thornycroft gearbox. Note the distinctive yellow, green and red flysheet; you could spot a Harris lorry miles away, especially when the sheets were new. (Photo: the author)

APPENDIX A

Auction Details And Bids

The first 100 lots were allocated to paraphernalia such as ropes, sheets, chains and tackle, spare parts, and tools etc. necessary to operate a road haulage business.

LOT NO.	DESCRIPTION	AMOUNT
110	1986 Tasker tri-axle 40ft. flat trailer, steel suspension. MoT expired. Ministry no. A.045635.	£1,000
111	1984 Crane Fruehauf tri-axle 40ft. flat trailer, steel suspension. MoT January 2002. Ministry no. A.020534.	£2,000
112	1984 Tasker tri-axle 40ft. flat trailer, steel suspension. MoT June 2001. Ministry no. A.013790.	£1,500
113	1985 Tasker tri-axle 40ft. flat trailer, steel suspension. MoT April 2001. Ministry no. A.024096.	£2,450
114	1986 Tasker tri-axle 40ft. flat trailer, steel suspension. MoT May 2001. Ministry no. A.048987.	£1,900
115	1986 Tasker tri-axle 40ft. flat trailer, steel suspension. MoT August 2001. Ministry no. A.039455.	£2,500
116	1986 Tasker tri-axle 40ft. flat trailer, steel suspension, MoT December 2001. Ministry no. A.042825.	£2,500
117	1988 Tasker tri-axle 40ft. flat trailer, steel suspension. MoT March 2002. Ministry no. A.059733.	£2,650
118	1988 Tasker tri-axle 40ft. flat trailer, steel suspension. MoT August 2001. Ministry no. A.067593.	£2,600
119	1988 Tasker tri-axle 40 ft. flat trailer, steel suspension. MoT December 2001. Ministry no. A.067254.	£2,800
120	1988 Whitehead tri-axle 40ft. PSK flat trailer, air suspension. MoT October 2001. Ministry no. A.0722453.	£2,900
121	1989 Crane Fruehauf 40ft. tri-axle flat trailer. MoT August 2001. Ministry no. A.064908.	£3,200
122	1989 Crane Fruehauf 40ft. tri-axle flat trailer. MoT August 2001. Ministry no. A.073834.	£4,000
123	1989 Crane Fruehauf 40ft. tri-axle PSK flat, air suspension. MoT January 2002. Ministry no. A.113117.	£3,800

LOT NO.	DESCRIPTION	AMOUNT
124	1991 Montracon 40ft. tri-axle PSK flat trailer, steel suspension. MoT January 2002. Ministry no. A.196435.	£3,400
125	1994 Dennison 40ft. tri-axle flat trailer, steel suspension. MoT September 2001. Ministry no. A.175618.	£3,400
126	1997 Tinsley 13.6m tri-axle Euroliner, Southfield body, sliding roof, front lift, air suspension. MoT expired, Ministry no. not recorded.	£7,600
127	1988 Tasker 40ft. tri-axle curtainsider trailer, air suspension. MoT December 2001. Ministry no. A.074101.	£1,500
128	1989 Montracon 40ft. tri-axle curtainsider trailer, air suspension. MoT February 2002. Ministry no. A.125559.	£2,050
129	1991 Crane Fruehauf 40ft. tri-axle curtainsider trailer, steel suspension. MoT November 2001. Ministry no. A.158551.	£2,900
130	1997 Crane Fruehauf 13.6m tri-axle curtainsider trailer, air suspension. MoT April 2001. Ministry no. A.242304.	£11,600
131	1998 Crane Fruehauf 13.6m tri-axle curtainsider trailer, air suspension. MoT August 2001. Ministry no. C.015562.	£10,300
132	1999 Crane Fruehauf 13.6m tri-axle curtainsider trailer, front lift, Roco body. MoT May 2001. Ministry no. C.011489.	£11,000
133	1986 Broshuis 40/60 tri-axle extendable trailer. MoT March 2002. Ministry no. A.039620.	£7,250
134	1995 ARB tri-axle plant low-loader trailer, rear lift, air suspension. MoT October 2001. Ministry no. A.213557.	£12,100
135	May 1990, G496 WDV, ERF E10.325 8x4 dropside tipper, sleeper cab. MoT May 2001.	£3,800
136	April 1994, L348 GDB, ERF EC10.325 8x4 alloy aggregates tipper. MoT October 2001.	£12,400
137	January 1996, N378 KHW, Seddon Atkinson L10.325, 4x2 unit, twin-splitter gearbox, day cab. MoT January 2002.	£3,000
138	September 1994, M255 PPY, Ford Transit 190D pick-up. MoT October 2001.	£2,900
139	October 1987, E416 KDC, Leyland 7.5 ton. MoT October 2001.	£1,000

LOT NO.	DESCRIPTION	AMOUNT
140	February 1993, K995 MGN, Leyland DAF 45.150, 7.5 ton, tail-lift, 18ft. body. MoT November 2001.	£2,400
141	? 1988, E802 DDV, ERF 4x2 shunter unit. MoT expired.	£1,050
142	October 1988, F248 XFL, ERF E14.320, 4x2 unit, sleeper cab. MoT March 2001, expired.	£950
143	November 1988, F377 HFJ, ERF E14.320, 4x2 unit, sleeper cab. MoT March 2002.	£1,050
144	March 1991, H78 CHW, ERF E10.325, 6x2 sleeper cab rigid. lift axle, 28ft. flat, 25 tonnes G.V.W. MoT June 2001.	£4,500
145	December 1995, Leyland DAF 65.210, sleeper cab 4x2 rigid. 25ft. flat, 18 tonnes G.V.W. MoT October 2001.	£5,800
146	May 1989, F513 MOD, ERF E14.320, 4x2 unit, sleeper cab. MoT June 2001.	£1,000
147	February 1989, F769 KOD, ERF E14.320, 4x2 unit, sleeper cab. MoT February 2002.	£1,050
148	September 1989, G901 STA, ERF E14.320, 4x2 unit, sleeper cab. MoT October 2001.	£1,500
149	February 1993, K151 GSO, ERF E14.410, 4x2 unit, sleeper cab, steel suspension, 3.8m wheelbase. MoT May 2001.	£1,750
150	November 1993, L419 RDM, ERF E14.380, 6x2 mid-lift unit, sleeper cab, steel suspension. MoT November 2001.	£4,000
151	November 1993, L769 KSS, ERF EC14.340 (uprated to 380), 6x2 rear steer unit, sleeper cab, steel suspension. MoT January 2001.	£3,000
152	September 1993, L965 NAO, ERF EC14.340 (uprated to 380), 6x2 rear steer, mid-lift conversion, unit, sleeper cab, steel suspension. MoT August 2001.	£3,800
153	December 1993, L278 RMB, ERF EC500, Celect 4x2 unit, air suspension, 3.8m wheelbase. MoT January 2002.	£8,100
154	August 1994, M448 VER, ERF EC14.340 (uprated to 380), 6x2 mid-lift unit, air suspension, tipping gear. MoT October 2001.	£7,000
155	September 1994, M672 YSW, ERF EC14.410, 6x2 rear steer unit, steel suspension. MoT March 2001.	£6,500

LOT NO.	DESCRIPTION	AMOUNT
156	June 1995, M913 YKF, ERF EC14.380, 4x2 unit, air suspension. MoT April 2001.	£5,000
157	October 1995, N155 TDV, ERF EC14.380, 4x2 unit, steel suspension. MoT October 2001.	£5,500
158	August 1996, P150 EFL, ERF EC14.380, 4x2 unit, air suspension, 3.8m wheelbase. MoT February 2002.	£8,000
159	December 1996, P970 BFJ, ERF EC14.380, 4x2 unit, steel suspension. MoT December 2001.	£7,800
160	August 1996, P680 YTT, ERF EC14.380, 4x2 unit, steel suspension. MoT August 2001.	£7,000
161	December 1997, R685 BDV, ERF EC11.380, 4x2 unit, steel suspension, RPC. MoT July 2001.	£12,000
162	August 1997, R450 PDV, ERF EC11.380, 4x2 unit, steel suspension, RPC. MoT April 2001.	£12,000
163	August 1998, S690 BTA, ERF EC11.380, 4x2 unit, steel suspension, extended warranty to 8/03, RPC. MoT June 2001.	£15,500
164	July 1999, T470 AFJ, ERF EC11.380, 4x2 unit, steel suspension, extended warranty to 7/04, RPC. MoT June 2001.	£20,000
165	August 1989, G403 OVM, ERF E14.400, 6x2 rear steer unit, fitted with Hiab 1165 crane. MoT January 2002.	£4,800
166	November 1994, M393 NNC, ERF E14.380, 6x2 rear steer unit, air suspension, fitted with 1997 Palfinger PF23080 crane. MoT September 2001.	£21,750
167	1960 ERF KV 4x2 dropside rigid, Gardner 5LW, 14 tons gvw. The vendor retained this lot, as it did not reach its reserve.	£5,250
168	1963 Thames Trader 4x2 dropside rigid in need of restoration. (Diesel storage tanks not included)	£250

APPENDIX B

Final Fleet List And Lorry Names

For many years every lorry carried a name, painted on a plate on the front grille. All these names had some reference to Dartmoor. Many names were used time and time again as vehicles were replaced and some drivers always drove a lorry bearing the same name. For instance Jimmy Webster had the 'Old Grey Mare' and whenever he had a new lorry it was named as such until he retired.

This list represents the fleet at the beginning of 2001, the final list at the time of closure.

ERF TRACTOR UNITS:

F248 FXL – Moorland Princess   F377 HFJ – Peter Davey
F513 MOD – Monarch Of The Moor   F762 KOD – Phantom Of The Moor
G403 OVM – Jan Stewer (Blue Livery)   G901 STA – Dartmoor Lady
K151 GSO – Knight Of The Moor   L278 RMB – King Of The Moor
L965 NAO – Dartmoor Viking   L769 KSS – Dartmoor Poacher
L419 RDM – Daniel Whiddon   M448 VER – Un-named
M393 NNC – Bill Brewer (Blue Livery) M913 YKF – Peter Gurney
M672 YSW – The Old Grey Mare   N155 TDV – Tom Pearce
P970 BFJ – Dartmoor Laddie (Blue Livery) P680 YTT – Dartmoor Lassie
P150 EFL – Dartmoor Crusader   R685 BDV – Widecombe Warrior
R450 PDV – Dartmoor Trooper   S690 BTA – Uncle Tom Cobley
T470 AFJ – Dartmoor Avenger

ERF 8-WHEEL TIPPERS:

G496 WDV – Widecombe Lad   L348 GDB – Happy Wanderer

ERF 6-WHEEL FLAT PLATFORM:

H78 CHW – Harry Hawke

LEYLAND DAF 4-WHEEL FLAT PLATFORM:

N169 TFJ – Uncle

LEYLAND DAF 7.5 TONNERS:

E416 KDC – Rugglestone Roamer   K995 MGN – Dartmoor Vixen

FORD TRANSIT:

M255 PPY – Rugglestone Rocket

On the day of the auction several of the lorries bore no nameplates as their drivers had been given them as mementoes when they left.

After publication of the first edition of this title in 2002 some other photographic material came to light as was to be expected. CDV 99C was new in 1965, an ERF LV cabbed tractor unit that carried the name 'Jan Stewer'. It was powered by a Gardner 6LX 150 engine. Here is was coupled to a new triple drop-side trailer. (photo: Brian Harris collection)

A 1965 Scammell Handyman tractor unit with Michelotti cab. Harris & Miners only operated two of these in its fleet. Once again another recent pictorial discovery. (photo: Brian Harris collection)

This was an ERF lorry that the author drove briefly in 1975. By then it was some four years old with a Gardner 6LXB 180 power unit. Its usual trailer was a 40-foot flat. (photo: John Henderson)

'Uncle Tom Cobley' or 222 TDV, photographed by Adrian Cypher in 1967. This was an unusual ERF LV with full length cab doors. It was also the first ERF artic on the Harris & Miners fleet in 1964. The precursor of many more that followed.

'Phantom of the Moor', ERF E Series F762 KOD was sold at the closure auction to a steam roller owner for pulling his low loader. Having since been sold on, it is now deteriorating in the open air on the Lizard peninsula in Cornwall (photo: R Allen)

Two pictures of 373 FOD. Firstly above, when it was new in 1960 and originally it was a 'distance' motor fitted with diesel tanks on both sides of the chassis. The off-side one was later removed when the vehicle was used on local deliveries in its later life as there was a Ministry man in Cornwall who was rather keen on the lorry not being overloaded. Below, the same lorry undergoing restoration at Boughey & Son, Much Wenlock, Shropshire. (photos: D. Brewer & John Corah)

373 FOD during its first preserved commercial vehicle rally since restoration, the 2005 Bournemouth to Colerne event where it won the best in class and best in show prizes. John Corah was the lucky driver for the road run, accompanied by Vic McCarthy, who took the upper photo at the Warminster rest stop. Below, John receiving the Best in Show trophy from the Mayor and Mayoress of Bath with run organiser John Pomeroy of Commercial Transport in Preservation announcing in the background.

A line-up of Harris & Miners / Brian Harris vehicles at Colerne, September 2005. The two in the centre never were part of the fleet but represent similar lorries that were run by the company; their respective owners had asked Brian if they could use his colours. The Albion however has been sold on recently and is no longer in the H & M livery. (photo Vic McCarthy)

Friday the 9th July 2002. The book launch of "From Moorlands To Highlands" at the Riverside Hotel, Bovey Tracey. Many smiling faces, all ex-drivers of the company line up in front of preserved ERF 'Monarch of the Moor'. The beer was already going down well! In the photo are from left to right: Richard Basson, Andy Pointon, Bill Baty, Ian Crook (electrician to the firm), Gary Ball, Norman 'Brummy' Piggot, Derek 'Soapy' Hudson, Peter Rees, Bill Mortimore, Brian Harris (partly hidden), Gordon Bamsey, Michael 'Bart' Bartholemew, John Corah, Bryn Jones, Colin 'Blacky' Black, John 'Grizzly' Liddicoat, Mick Whiteway, Alf Harvey, Eric Whiteway. (photo: John Corah collection)

F377 HFJ 'Peter Davey', an ERF F14 from 1989 languishing in a mid-Devon scrap yard. Driven by Bryn Jones for Brian Harris but unlikely to be driven by him or anyone else ever again. The owner wants £3,000 for it! Peter Wygell, who took this picture, says it would need a complete rebuild and the cab interior is ruined because of the missing headboard. The resulting ingress of rainwater has seen to that.

'Dartmoor Lassie' is now owned by Peter Wright of Bideford, North Devon, to pull his Burnell Showman's tractor on a Taskers trailer. He keeps this ex-Brian Harris ERF in beautiful condition and it has recently been repainted in its original livery. Jerry Snell drove it when new. (photo: Brian Harris collection)

Signwriter John Corah has signwritten this tractor unit four times; twice for Brian, once for Bryn Jones who ran it in his own colours as an owner-driver and recently for Clint Mooney from Strood in Kent who has returned the ERF into its original blue livery. The only preserved blue one and driven all the way from Kent to Devon for an authentic signwriting job. Thank you Clint and also for the picture.